Love your Leftovers

Love your Leftovers

You call it leftovers - we call it ingredients

This edition published by Parragon Books Ltd in 2013
LOVE FOOD is an imprint of Parragon Books Ltd

Parragon Books Ltd
Chartist House
15-17 Trim Street
Bath BA1 1HA, UK
www.parragon.com

ISBN 978-1-4723-3403-9

Printed in China

The visual index is a registered design registered with the European Trademark Office under the number 000252796-001

Text: Gerhard von Richthofen, Günter Beer
Recipes and home economist: Patrik Jaros
Photography: Günter Beer
Produced by Buenavista Studio S.L.
Design by Cammaert & Eberhardt

Notes for the Reader
This book uses both metric and imperial measurements. Follow the same units of measurement throughout; do not mix metric and imperial. All spoon measurements are level: teaspoons are assumed to be 5 ml, and tablespoons are assumed to be 15 ml. Unless otherwise stated, milk is assumed to be full fat, eggs and individual vegetables are medium, and pepper is freshly ground black pepper. Unless otherwise stated, all root vegetables should be washed in plain water and peeled prior to using.

For best results, use a food thermometer when cooking meat and poultry – check the latest government guidelines for current advice. Garnishes, decorations andserving suggestions are all optional and not necessarily included in the recipe ingredients or method.

The times given are an approximate guide only. Preparation times differ according to the techniques used by different people and the cooking times may also vary from those given. Optional ingredients, variations or serving suggestions have not been included in the time calculations.

Recipes using raw or very lightly cooked eggs should be avoided by infants, the elderly, pregnant women, convalescents and anyone suffering from an illness. Pregnant and breastfeeding women are advised to avoid eating peanuts and peanut products. Sufferers from nut allergies should be aware that some of the ready-made ingredients used in the recipes in this book may contain nuts. Always check the packaging before use.

Vegetarians should be aware that some of the ready-made ingredients used in the recipes in this book may contain animal products. Always check the packaging before use.

This book contains recipes where leftover food is used. However, if you are not sure that the food is in perfect condition, you should definitely throw it away and not use it. Always keep leftover food in a refrigerator and carefully check its condition before use. On no account should spoiling food be eaten. Take particular care when eating leftover rice. Rice must be chilled quickly after cooking and may be kept in the refrigerator for one day at most and thoroughly reheated before being used again.

Contents

How this cookbook works

The illustrated **list of ingredients** at the top of the left-hand page can be used as a quick index. Without having to read the book, you can find recipes for one, two or several ingredients in a flash.

The stars indicate the level of difficulty: one star for easy, two for medium difficulty, three stars for difficult.

The **numbers** at the bottom of each recipe indicate the approximate preparation time in minutes.

This book assumes that the following ingredients are available in all kitchens and therefore lists them only if larger quantities are needed: butter, vegetable oil, olive oil, red and white wine vinegar, sugar, salt, pepper.

Recipes are for two people, unless stated otherwise.

Some time at the beginning of this millennium, the chef Patrik Jaros and the food photographer Günter Beer decided to produce a brand-new type of cookbook. A cookbook for the small kitchens of the 21st century, for the single person; a book that could be used every day and be understood by an amateur cook; a book that only used ingredients that would be in the house anyway.

This book is the result. It contains many brand-new recipes never seen before and uses leftovers, which we always get wherever food is cooked and eaten.

It presents well-known ingredients in completely new combinations. It makes use of takeaway cuisine, of which most of us partake at some time or other, as a source of unusual creations. And it uses prepared foods off the supermarket shelves, making them into surprisingly fine dishes with very little effort.

However, the true ingredient of this book is imagination. Imagination that serves popcorn with chocolate, turns canned sardines into a sandwich spread and prepares cornflakes (without milk) in a frying pan.

If you like experimenting and trying things out, you will surprise yourself – and others – with your culinary talent.

Preparation in jars and cans

Dirty bowls and plates?
Use jars and cans!

Is your sink stacked with dirty dishes and your crockery cupboard bare? Not a problem for today's single person. Why mess up plates when food comes in jars anyway? Instead of pots, you can use cans and containers.

Why add dressing to the salad if the salad will fit into the dressing? Prepared in the jar, it can be eaten out of the jar as well. This not only saves time, it also tastes better.

 1 tbsp honey

1/2 bottle ketchup
(about 200 ml/7 fl oz)

2 tsp curry powder

1 tbsp Worcestershire sauce

1 tbsp brandy

Barbecue sauce
Ketchup and honey sauce

1. Pour the honey into the ketchup bottle.

2. Add the curry powder.

3. Now pour in the Worcestershire sauce.

4. And finally, add the brandy. Close the bottle tightly and...

5. Shake well!

Halve a bread roll, add a hot-dog sausage and garnish with barbecue sauce. According to taste, add a little mustard, a few slices of sour gherkin and a little chopped onion.

Preparation in jars and cans

 10

- Will keep in the refrigerator for about a month. Ideal for summer barbecues.
**Not suitable for children.
Shake before use.**

3

4

5

1

2

Mustard dip for salad and crudités
Make the best of leftover mustard

Don't throw away that jar with leftover mustard. The dried-on mustard can be used to make a wonderful salad dressing:

1. Add ¹/₂ teaspoon of salt.

2. Add ¹/₂ teaspoon of ground black pepper.

3. Add a few splashes of vinegar.

4. Double the resulting amount by adding olive oil.

5. Close the jar tightly and shake well. This also loosens the leftover mustard from the sides of the jar, and all the mustard is then added to the sauce.

Pour the finished mustard dressing into little bowls and serve with cherry or baby plum tomatoes and endive leaves.

Preparation in jars and cans

* * * 10

■ **Add a little lukewarm water to make the dressing less intense and acidic in flavour.**

3

4

5

250 g (9 oz) full-fat yogurt

1 tsp paprika (sweet)

1 tbsp pesto

1

2

Pesto and yogurt dip for vegetable sticks
Yogurt de luxe

1. Place the yogurt in a clean screw-top jar and add the paprika.

2. Now add the pesto and season with salt and pepper.

3. Finally, pour in 2 tablespoons of good-quality olive oil and close the lid of the jar.

4. Now shake the jar well, until all the ingredients are thoroughly mixed.

   Pour into small bowls and serve with vegetable sticks, radishes or cherry tomatoes for dipping.

Preparation in jars and cans

* * * **10**

■ Instead of pesto, you could use green or black olive tapenade to make the dip taste even spicier.

3

4

1 small clove of garlic

 1/2 jar of cooked chickpeas in brine (250 g/9 oz)

 1 tbsp sesame seeds

 1 tsp toasted sesame oil

1

2

Hummus prepared in a jar
Fresh & easy hummus

1. Peel the clove of garlic and slice thinly. Add to the chickpeas.

2. Also add 1 tablespoon of red wine vinegar to the jar.

3. Now add the sesame seeds and the sesame oil.

4. Pour in 2 tablespoons of olive oil and season with freshly ground salt and pepper.

5. Mix in the jar using a hand-held stick blender.

Pour onto a plate or into a bowl and, finally, according to taste, drizzle with olive oil and sprinkle with sesame seeds. Best of all, serve with lightly toasted strips of bread - good for dipping into the hummus.

Preparation in jars and cans

✳
✳ 5
✳

■ Add a special flavour to the hummus with tahini (sesame-seed paste).

3

4

5

1 tbsp green peppercorns in brine

 1 jar of asparagus (250 g/9 oz)

2 tbsp chopped celery leaves

1

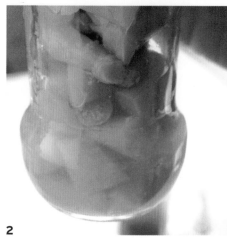

2

White asparagus salad with green peppercorns
Shake 'em, baby

1. Roughly crush the peppercorns with the back of a knife.

2. Remove the asparagus from the jar and cut the stems into 3-cm (1 1/4-inch) chunks. Pour off the asparagus liquid except for the last 3 cm (1 1/4 inch). Put the asparagus chunks back into the jar.

3. Add 2 tablespoons of red wine vinegar or blackcurrant vinegar to the asparagus.

4. Add the crushed peppercorns, the finely chopped celery leaves and 3 tablespoons of olive oil to the chopped asparagus.

5. Put the lid on the jar and shake carefully.

Pour the salad from the jar onto a plate and serve with slices of toast.

Preparation in jars and cans

10

3

4

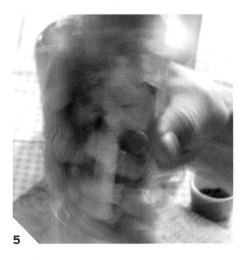

5

3/4 jar of cooked potato slices in juice (400 g/14 oz)

 10 cherry tomatoes

1 tbsp chopped parsley

 1 tsp curry powder

 3 tbsp mayonnaise

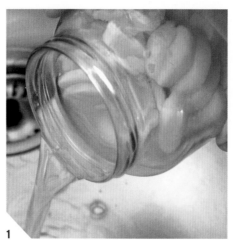

1

2

Quick potato salad with cherry tomatoes and mayonnaise
Shaken not stirred

1. Pour off all the juice from the cooked potato slices.

2. Add halved cherry tomatoes, chopped parsley, freshly ground black pepper and curry powder to the potato slices in the jar.

3. Now add the mayonnaise.

4. Finally, add 2 tablespoons of red wine vinegar.

5. Simply put the lid back on the jar and shake lightly to finish preparing the potato salad.

Tip the salad out of the jar straight onto the plate and, as a final touch, sprinkle over a little more curry powder.

Preparation in jars and cans

* * * 10

3

4

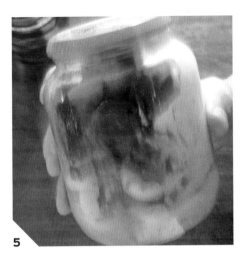

5

2 tbsp ketchup

 1/2 jar mayonnaise (125 g/4 1/2 oz)

 1 tbsp freshly pressed orange juice

 1 tsp brandy

 300 g (10 1/2 oz) cooked chicken

200 g (7 oz) canned pineapple slices

1

2

Cocktail dressing for chicken salad
Retro dressing

1. Put the ketchup into the jar with the mayonnaise.

2. Add the orange juice. If you have a little orange juice left over from breakfast, you can use that.

3. Add a shot of brandy. Don't use rum!

4. Close the jar tightly and keep shaking.

5. Cut up the remains of the cooked chicken, removing the skin. Cut up the pineapple rings and mix both with the cocktail dressing. Season with salt and black pepper.

Serve in small bowls garnished with lettuce leaves, slices of orange and a sprinkling of paprika.

Preparation in jars and cans

 **10**

■ **This allows you to make the best use of leftovers and to keep the remaining cocktail dressing in the tightly closed jar for another occasion.**

3

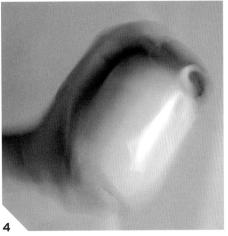

4

5

1 leek

1 carrot

$1/2$ jar of cooked lentils
(300 g/10$1/2$ oz)

1 tsp fine-quality mustard

2 tbsp balsamic vinegar

1

2

Lentil salad with diced vegetables prepared in the jar

Fast food with crudités

1. Halve the leek, wash well and then cut lengthways into long strips.

2. Now dice the strips of leek finely. Watch your fingers, especially your thumb!

3. Peel the carrot, cut it lengthways into thin slices, then into strips, and dice the strips finely. Add to the jar of lentils, together with the diced leek.

4. Then add mustard, a pinch of salt and black pepper, and the balsamic vinegar to the jar of lentils and close the lid.

5. Prepare the salad, mixing it in the jar by shaking lightly.

   Serve in bowls with lightly toasted bread.

Preparation in jars and cans

3

4

5

Preserving

You know the scene: you go to the supermarket hungry and come out still hungry but with enough food to last for weeks.

What to do? Eat until you burst? Feed it to the cat or the goldfish? Donate it to charity? Compost it? Or put it straight into the rubbish?

Why not try preserving, and at the same time improving, your excess food? There are many methods: boiling, freezing, pickling, marinating – in sugar, vinegar, oil or alcohol. You can vary the flavours according to your choice: sweet, sour, sweet-sour. Improved flavour and durability included!

1 clove of garlic

 1 bunch of basil

 2 tbsp pine nuts

 90 ml (3 fl oz) olive oil

50 g (1³/₄ oz) finely grated Parmesan cheese

1

2

Basil pesto with pine nuts and olive oil
Basil forever

1. Peel the clove of garlic, chop into small pieces and crush with a pestle and mortar and add a pinch of salt.

2. Add the washed basil leaves and the pine nuts and crush finely with the olive oil.

3. Add the Parmesan cheese and continue to work on the mixture.

4. Once the basil pesto is finely ground and nicely creamy, adjust the seasoning with salt and pepper and keep in a closed jar in the refrigerator.

You can leave the pesto a little coarser, which adds to that home-made flavour. The pesto will keep for a good 4 weeks in the refrigerator.

Preserving

■ **Shortly before serving, pour the pesto onto the freshly cooked pasta and mix it in. This is the best way to allow the flavour to develop.**

3

4

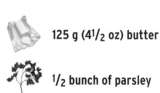 125 g (4½ oz) butter

 ½ bunch of parsley

 1 small clove of garlic

 1 spring onion

1 tsp spicy mustard

A few drops of Tabasco sauce

1

2

Herb butter with onions and spicy mustard
Steak-house style

1. Put the butter in a bowl and leave to soften at room temperature. Do not throw the wrapper of the butter away.

2. Wash the parsley well, shake it dry and chop it finely. Also chop the garlic and spring onion finely and add these to the butter. Add the spicy mustard.

3. Season with a dash or two of Tabasco sauce and salt and black pepper.

4. Mix the ingredients well, using a fork.

5. Place the finished herb butter on the butter wrapper. Shape into a roll and place in the refrigerator.

Cut the herb butter into slices, place these on grilled pork steaks and serve with grilled potatoes. The herb butter will last for 4 weeks in the freezer compartment.

Preserving

15

- If you don't have any herbs handy, you can use a tablespoon of tomato purée instead. This gives the butter a lovely red colour and will go well with grilled fish.

3

4

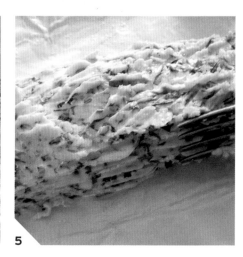

5

500 g (1 lb 2 oz) tomatoes

 1 orange

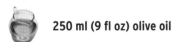 3 sprigs of thyme

250 ml (9 fl oz) olive oil

1

2

Dried tomato slices with orange peel and thyme
After the tomato harvest

1. Wash the tomatoes, cut them into ½ cm (¼ inch) thick slices and place them on a baking tray.

2. Sprinkle the tomatoes with salt, black pepper and 2 tablespoons of sugar. Drizzle with 2 tablespoons of olive oil.

3. Remove a couple of pieces of peel from the orange with a peeler and cut these into thin strips. Scatter over the tomatoes together with the thyme sprigs and place in the oven, preheated to 80°C (175°F/on the lowest setting).

4. Leave the tomatoes in the oven for 1 hour and then turn off the oven. It's best to leave the tomatoes to cool in the oven overnight.

5. Put the tomatoes into jars and pour over enough oil to cover them. They will keep like this for at least 1 month in the refrigerator.

Mix the tomato slices into pasta, together with the oil, and sprinkle with Parmesan cheese. They also taste good on a base of salad or slices of fresh mozzarella.

Preserving

✳
✳ 90
✳

■ **You can use a potato peeler to shave off even pieces of cheese and use these for decoration.**

3

4

5

½ pineapple

 2 onions

 85 g (3 oz) flaked almonds

 2 tsp curry powder

 150 g (5½ oz) brown sugar

 100 ml (3½ fl oz) white wine vinegar

1

2

Pineapple and onion chutney with flaked almonds and curry powder

Pineapple in a jar

1. Peel the pineapple and cut out the 'eyes'. Then dice the pineapple.

2. Peel the onions, cut into strips and fry lightly in oil. Add the flaked almonds, curry powder, sugar and ½ a teaspoon of salt.

3. Add the diced pineapple.

4. Pour on the white wine vinegar and leave to simmer gently for around 30 minutes.

5. The chutney is ready when nearly all the liquid has been absorbed and the chutney tastes nice and spicy and sweet-sour. Now pour it – still hot is best – into jars with lids and leave to cool. In the refrigerator, the chutney will keep in a closed jar for a good 2-3 months.

This chutney tastes best served with thin slices of strong cheese.

Preserving

✳
✳ 60
✳

■ Peel the pineapple and remove the 'eyes' lengthways with a knife.

1 small cauliflower

 200 ml (7 fl oz) white wine vinegar

 120 g (4¼ oz) sugar

 1 red chilli

 1 tbsp mixed peppercorns

 2 cloves of garlic with peel

 3 carrots

1

Cauliflower and carrot pickle
Vegetable pickle

1. Cut the cauliflower florets off the stalk with a small knife.

2. Put 500 ml (18 fl oz) of water and the vinegar, sugar, chilli, peppercorns and cloves of garlic into a saucepan and bring to the boil. Peel the carrots, cut them into diagonal slices and add them to the saucepan.

3. Add the cauliflower florets and leave to boil for 5 minutes. Then take the saucepan off the heat.

4. Pour into jars with lids while the mixture is still hot and cover completely with the liquid.

5. Close the jars and allow them to cool. It's best to leave the pickles for a few days to allow the flavours to blend properly, letting the cauliflower and carrots marinate fully in the spicy liquid.

   These mixed pickles can be kept for 4 weeks in the refrigerator if the lid is tightly closed.

Preserving

- Serve the sweet-sour cauliflower and carrots with salami, ham or pâté, together with fresh bread.

2 cucumbers

3 cloves of garlic

1 red chilli

1

2

Marinated cucumber with garlic and chilli

Cucumber, medium hot

1. Peel the cucumbers so that some strips of the peel remain. Quarter them lengthways and remove the seeds.

2. Then chop into smaller pieces, place in a bowl and mix with the thinly sliced garlic and chilli.

3. Sprinkle 1 tablespoon of sugar and 1 tablespoon of salt over the cucumbers.

4. Now pour over 2 tablespoons of white wine vinegar and mix. Cover and leave in the refrigerator for a day, allowing the cucumbers to marinate thoroughly. The cucumbers will keep in the marinade for a good week – they will get more and more spicy!

This dish goes well with grilled or fried pork and also makes a good snack with beer.

Preserving

15

3

4

 **2 bunches of flat-leaf parsley**

1

2

Parsley cubes for soups and sauces
Parsley power

1. Pluck the parsley leaves off the stems and wash well in cold water. Take them out of the water, place in a sealable freezer bag and pour off the rest of the water.

2. Sealed in the bag, the slightly damp parsley will keep in the refrigerator for several days, as if it had just been freshly picked.

3. Alternatively, chop the parsley finely with a large, sharp knife.

4. Put the chopped parsley into the ice cube tray and fill with water. Place in the freezer.

5. Break out the frozen ice cubes when needed and just add to a soup or sauce to dissolve.

The parsley cubes will keep in the freezer compartment for at least 3 months. You'll always have fresh parsley handy!

Preserving

 **15**

- **Don't throw the parsley stalks away, as they can also be used for seasoning - tie in a bunch with kitchen string and add to sauces or soups.**

3

4

5

500 ml (18 fl oz) white wine vinegar or fruit vinegar

100 g (3½ oz) redcurrants

2 tbsp brown sugar

1

2

Home-made redcurrant vinegar

Redcurrants in vinegar

1. Put the vinegar into a small saucepan and add the redcurrants.

2. Sprinkle in the sugar and bring to the boil.

3. Allow the vinegar and the redcurrants to simmer for 1 minute and then remove from the heat.

4. Pour through a sieve into a pot.

5. Squeeze as many of the redcurrants as possible through the sieve by pressing them with a small ladle. This will intensify the flavour of the vinegar. Pour the vinegar into a bottle and close. It will keep like this for 6 months.

Mix a dressing using this vinegar, olive oil, salt, pepper and sugar and pour over a leafy salad.

Preserving

✳
✳
✳ 15

■ Instead of using redcurrants, you can make a very spicy herb vinegar using thyme and peppercorns.

3

4

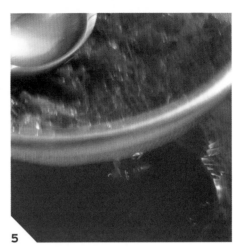

5

2-3 large sprigs of rosemary

 2 sprigs of thyme

 3 bay leaves

 a few stalks of parsley

 3 cloves of garlic with peel

 500 ml (18 fl oz) olive oil

1

2

Herb olive oil with rosemary, bay and thyme

Herb oil made easy

1. Put the sprigs of rosemary and thyme into a dry bottle.

2. Add the bay leaves and stalks of parsley to the bottle.

3. Lightly crush the cloves of garlic in their peel and add to the bottle.

4. Heat the olive oil slightly. When the oil starts forming a streaky pattern, it's at the right temperature.

5. Using a funnel, pour the oil into the bottle and leave to cool. The oil will become slightly cloudy due to the herbs and the cooling process, but this will clear again after a while. The herb oil will keep for 1 month.

Drizzle the herb oil over ripe tomatoes with red onion rings and a little celery. The oil's flavour will be at its best in simple dishes such as this.

Preserving

■ After cooling, it's best to keep the oil in the refrigerator - the aroma will last longer.

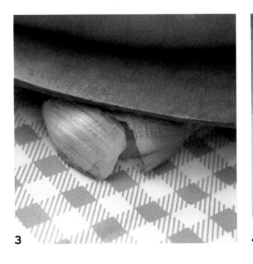

3

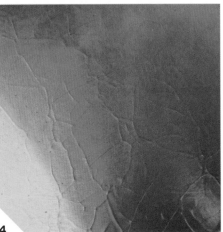

4

5

1 skinless chicken breast

 1 spring onion

 1 tsp apricot jam

 1 tbsp pistachio nuts

 1 tbsp port or sherry

Preserved chicken breast with pistachios
Chicken in a jam jar

1. Cut the chicken breast into small pieces and roughly chop the spring onion. Put both into a bowl with the apricot jam.

2. Mix in the pistachio nuts, port or sherry, and season with salt and black pepper.

3. Put the mixture into a clean jam jar and press down lightly with a spoon.

4. Screw the lid onto the jar. Put some paper towels in the base of a saucepan, then fill with enough water to cover the jar. Bring to the boil, then reduce the heat. Carefully place the jar on top of the paper towels (these will keep the jar in place whilst cooking) and simmer gently for 45 minutes.

5. Remove the jar from the water and leave to cool to room temperature. Store in the refrigerator. This simple pâté will last for a good 2 weeks.

Serve with toast and pickled vegetables.

Preserving

 60

3

4

5

300 g (10¹/₂ oz) salmon fillet without the skin

 1 red onion

 2 carrots

1 celery stick

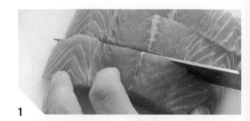 100 ml (3¹/₂ fl oz) white wine vinegar

 1 tbsp mixed crushed peppercorns

 2 bay leaves

1

2

Raw salmon cooked in hot vegetable marinade

Bay leaf salmon

1. First cut the salmon fillet into 2-cm (³/₄-inch) strips, then into cubes of the same size. Put into a deep baking dish.

2. Peel and quarter the onion and cut it into strips. Peel the carrots and cut them and the celery stick into diagonal slices.

3. Put 500 ml (18 fl oz) of water, 3 tablespoons of sugar, the vinegar, vegetables, peppercorns and bay leaves into a saucepan and bring to the boil.

4. Let the marinade boil for some 5 minutes and then leave to cool.

5. When the marinade is still very hot, pour it over the salmon cubes and then allow these to marinate in the refrigerator for at least 1 hour, overnight if possible. The marinated fish, if kept cool, will keep for 3–5 days.

Serve the salmon in bowls or deep plates with the marinade, along with Swedish crispbread with plenty of butter.

Preserving

 95

■ Do you have any other fish in the refrigerator? Fresh tuna, perhaps, or soused herring fillets or trout fillets? The marinade will taste great with these fish as well.

3

4

5

4 chicken thighs

 10 cloves of garlic with peel

 1 sprig of rosemary

 1 tbsp coarse mustard

 200 ml (7 fl oz) dry white wine

 200 g (7 oz) potatoes

1

Chicken in mustard and white wine marinade with whole cloves of garlic

Chicken revived

1. Halve the chicken thighs and mix them with the cloves of garlic (crushed in their peel), the rosemary, mustard and white wine. Leave to marinate.

2. Drizzle with 3 tablespoons of olive oil and put in the refrigerator for at least 1 or 2 hours. You can also marinate the chicken for up to 3 days. This means it will keep for longer.

3. Put the chicken thighs with the marinade in a ceramic baking dish and add the peeled and roughly chopped potatoes. Now bake in the preheated oven at about 200°C (400°F/Gas Mark 6) for 45 minutes. Turn the chicken thighs occasionally if necessary.

Put the baking dish with the chicken thighs on the table and allow people to help themselves.

Preserving

 130

■ **To get the last traces of mustard out of the jar, pour in wine, shake the jar and then pour it over the meat.**

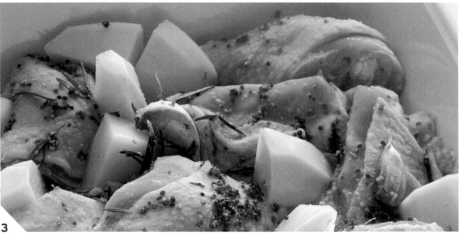

500 g (1 lb 2 oz) root vegetables such as carrots, celery and onions

 1 clove of garlic

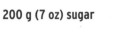 200 g (7 oz) sugar

 200 ml (7 fl oz) white wine vinegar

1 tsp juniper berries

 3 bay leaves

 1-1.5 kg (2 lb 4 oz-3 lb 5 oz) braising beef

 1 tbsp tomato purée

 300 ml (10 fl oz) cream

1

Sweet-sour roast in vegetable sauce

Sweet & sour beef pot roast

1. Cut the vegetables into small pieces and chop the whole clove of garlic in half. Pour 2 litres (3^1/$_2$ pints) of water into a saucepan and bring to the boil with the sugar, vinegar, juniper berries, bay leaves, vegetables and garlic. Simmer for 5 minutes and leave to cool.

2. Put the meat into a pot and pour the marinade over it.

3. Marinate for 5 days. Take out the meat and leave it to drain on paper towels. Strain the marinade through a sieve, reserving the vegetables and liquid.

Season the meat with salt and pepper and brown in a large pot. Add the reserved vegetables, juniper berries, bay leaves and garlic and fry these too. Add the tomato purée and pour in the marinade. Cover and simmer gently for 2 hours, turning occasionally.

Take out the meat, add the cream to the sauce and mix. Strain the sauce through a fine sieve and put the meat back in the sauce for serving.

This pot roast will feed 4-6 people.

Preserving

■ **You can keep meat in a marinade for 3-5 days in the refrigerator. The meat also becomes wonderfully tender.**

3 oranges

 1 lime

 300 g (10½ oz) sugar

 8 star anise

 8 cardamom pods

1

2

Spiced orange syrup
Tea with oranges

1. Wash the oranges and lime well under hot water and then cut into 3-cm (1-inch) cubes.

2. Put 750 ml (1⅓ pints) of water and the chopped citrus fruit into a saucepan. Add the sugar, star anise and cardamom pods.

3. Leave to simmer gently for about 30 minutes, stirring occasionally, removing the scum forming on the surface with a slotted spatula. Leave to cool for a little while afterwards and then pour into jars that can be tightly closed.

   This syrup will keep for at least 3 months.

Preserving

60

3

1 litre (1³/₄ pints) milk

400 g (14 oz) sugar

1

Caramelized milk
Home-made caramel toast

1. Put the milk and the sugar into a saucepan and bring to the boil slowly.

2. Remove the scum that forms on the surface with a small ladle to make sure that the sweetened milk contains no lumps later.

3. The sweet milk is ready when it is a nice caramel colour and is just starting to become viscous. Now pour it into a jar, close and leave to cool. The caramelized milk will keep for at least 3 months.

Toast slices of fresh white bread and spread with this 'dulce de leche' – a classic breakfast in Argentina.

Preserving

∗
∗ 50
∗

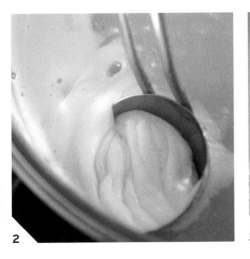

500 g (1 lb 2 oz) frozen berries

 4 tbsp brown sugar

 500 ml (18 fl oz) dark or light rum

1

Fruit in rum
Tipsy berries

1. Put the frozen berries into a bowl, mix with brown sugar and leave to stand for 5 minutes.

2. Put the sugared berries into a tall glass or beaker.

3. Now pour rum over the fruit until all the berries are covered. Then, if possible, put a lid on and keep in a cool dark place.

Thanks to the alcohol and sugar, the fruit will keep for a good 3 months. Simply sprinkle these rum-soaked fruits over vanilla ice cream or serve with sweet pancakes. But watch the portions – after a while the little fruits acquire quite a kick!

There is enough fruit in this recipe for 4-6 people.

Preserving

 10

2

3

4 pears

 200 ml (7 fl oz) white wine

 100 g (3^1/$_2$ oz) sugar

2 sticks of cinnamon

 3 lemon slices

 1 tsp coffee beans

 5 cloves

1

Compote of pears with coffee beans and cinnamon
Hard pears gone soft

1. Wash the pears and peel them so as to leave little strips of peel on the fruit.

2. Quarter the pears and cut out the cores with a knife.

3. Pour 300 ml (10 fl oz) of water into a saucepan and bring to the boil with the white wine and the sugar. Add the quartered pears.

4. Now add the cinnamon sticks, slices of lemon, coffee beans and cloves. Cover and leave to simmer gently for about 20 minutes.

5. To check whether the pears are cooked through, test the pieces with a knife. If the pears are very ripe, the cooking time will of course be shorter. Leave them to cool in their own juice.

Now pour the pear compote into pudding bowls and serve. The compote will keep for 2 weeks in the refrigerator.

Preserving

✳
✳ 40
✳

 **4 oranges**

 **3 tbsp Campari**

1

2

Campari and orange sorbet
Aperitif for pudding

1. Squeeze the oranges. Pour the juice into a tall container and add 3 tablespoons of sugar.

2. Stir in the Campari.

3. Scrape out the squeezed orange halves with a small teaspoon until only the white inner peel is left.

4. Place the scraped orange halves side by side in a shallow dish so that they cannot fall over. Fill with the orange juice mixture and place in the freezer compartment for 3 hours.

To serve, perk up the orange halves with half a slice of orange and an extra shot of Campari.

This Campari and orange sorbet recipe will serve 4 people. It will keep for a good 3 months in the freezer compartment.

Preserving

✳
✳ 200
✳

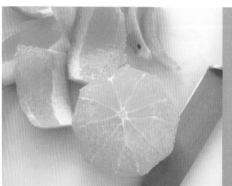

■ **To loosen the orange from the peel, use a knife to remove the peel from the orange together with the white pith. Then slice the fruit and use for decoration.**

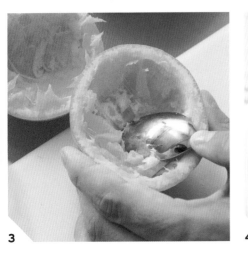

3

4

500 g (1 lb 2 oz) full-fat yogurt

 150 g (5½ oz) blueberries

 4 tbsp caster sugar

1 **2**

Creamy yogurt and blueberry ice lollies
Blueberries on a stick

1. Put the yogurt and blueberries into a blender.

2. Sprinkle with the caster sugar.

3. Blend slowly until all the ingredients are well mixed.

4. The mixture is ready when the blueberries are finely puréed and the yogurt is an intense purple colour.

5. Now pour the mixture into ice-lolly moulds and put into the freezer compartment for a good 3 hours.

This makes a lovely pudding – sweet and refreshing at the same time.

The mixture makes enough blueberry ice lollies for 7 people and will keep in the freezer compartment for 3 months.

Preserving

185

3   4   5

200 g (7 oz) strawberries

 6 tbsp caster sugar

1

2

Strawberry ice
Strawberry fields forever

1. Select over-ripe strawberries and use a knife to hull them.

2. Put the strawberries in a measuring jug and sprinkle with the caster sugar. Process to a purée using a hand-held stick blender.

3. Place the mixture in a shallow bowl and put into the freezer compartment.

4. Leave to freeze for about 2 hours, occasionally stirring the mixture to prevent the ice from forming a single block.

Put the ice into chilled glasses and finally pour over some light cream.

This strawberry ice recipe makes enough for 4 and will keep for 3 months in the freezer compartment.

Preserving

✳
✳ 130
✳

■ **Also makes a good ice lolly. Put the strawberry mixture into the appropriate moulds, add the stick and wait...**

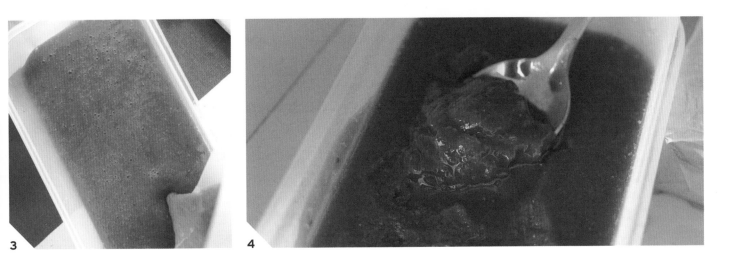

3

4

2 sprigs of rosemary

 500 ml (18 fl oz) milk

 500 ml (18 fl oz) cream

 3 tbsp honey

1 egg

1

Rosemary and honey ice cream

A scoop of rosemary, please

1. Strip the rosemary leaves off the stalk and chop in a blender together with 3 tablespoons of sugar.

2. Pour the milk, cream and rosemary sugar into a tall container.

3. Now add the honey.

4. Finally, add the egg and beat until foamy. Pour the mixture into small moulds and put into the freezer compartment for 2^1/$_2$-3 hours.

Either serve the ice cream in the moulds or tip out onto a plate before serving.

This makes enough rosemary and honey ice cream for 4 people and will keep for 3 months in the freezer compartment.

Preserving

■ **Try rosemary sugar to sweeten your tea. It tastes fantastic and also has a calming effect.**

2

3

4

 1 bunch of mint

 100 g (3¹/₂ oz) sugar

250 g (9 oz) strawberries

1

2

Mint sugar with strawberries
After-party mojito

1. Remove any shrivelled mint leaves and keep these for making tea. Put the best and most tender leaves in water so that they do not wither and put them aside.

2. Use the average-quality leaves for making the mint sugar.

3. Process the mint leaves with the sugar in a blender until the leaves are chopped very finely and the sugar is light green in colour. Then transfer to a jar with a lid and keep in the refrigerator. The mint sugar will keep for at least 3 months like this.

You can sweeten and decorate the strawberries at the same time with plenty of mint sugar.

Preserving

✳
✳
✳ 15

■ Put the mint leaves in a glass and pour on hot water. Mint tea is esteemed in Arab countries for its refreshing effect.

3

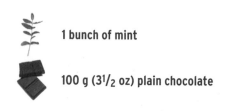

1 bunch of mint

100 g (3¹/₂ oz) plain chocolate

1

2

Mint leaves in chocolate
Home-made after-dinner mints

1. Pluck the mint leaves off the stalks.

2. Break the chocolate into small pieces, put them in a heatproof bowl over a saucepan of gently simmering water and heat until melted. Place the mint leaves on a sheet of baking paper.

3. Drip a little chocolate onto each mint leaf.

4. Spread the chocolate over the mint leaves with a knife and allow to cool.

The chocolate mint leaves will keep in the refrigerator for 1 week.

Preserving

40

■ It would be a shame to leave the remains of the chocolate in the saucepan. Add some milk and bring to the boil, stirring constantly. The chocolate will dissolve in the milk, and your drinking chocolate is ready.

3

4

Good yesterday, better today

You've made a new friend at the cinema, or you've met an old school friend in the bar, and you need to make more of the occasion. But how?

An impromptu dinner invitation, of course! But that's hardly possible without going shopping first, and certainly not on a Saturday night. Or perhaps it is. How about cheese-topped tortilla chips bought at the cinema or yesterday's gnocchi with red curry sauce? And perhaps a cocoa sorbet to go with it? It'll undoubtedly make for an unforgettable evening.

200 g (7 oz) plain flour

 1 egg

 3 tsp black peppercorns

 150 ml (5 fl oz) beer

 300 g (10½ oz) frozen squid rings in batter

 1 litre (2 pints) oil for deep frying

1

2

Squid rings in pepper batter
Double-battered squid

1. Put the flour, egg and crushed peppercorns into a bowl.

2. Carefully stir in the beer, adding it little by little.

3. The mix is at the right consistency when it runs off a fork.

4. Put the frozen squid into the batter mixture and turn the rings to make sure they are fully coated.

5. Heat the oil in a medium-depth saucepan. Add the squid rings and turn them with a wooden skewer.

When the rings are golden yellow, transfer them to paper towels to drain.

Serve with rémoulade sauce and wedges of lemon.

Good yesterday, better today

✳ ✳ ✳ 25

■ Crush the peppercorns carefully, using a pestle, so that they don't jump away when pressed.

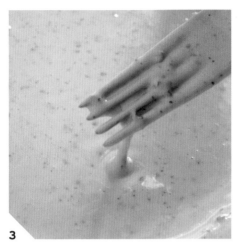

3

4

5

6 sushi rolls

 1 tsp toasted sesame oil

 1 tbsp oyster sauce

 1 tsp chopped fresh coriander

1

Fried sushi in sesame oil
Yesterday's sushi, part I

1. Place yesterday's sushi rolls in a hot non-stick frying pan, drizzle with sesame oil and fry for 1 minute.

2. Pour the oyster sauce around the sushi and let it spread in the hot pan.

3. Now turn the sushi and fry for another minute on the other side.

4. Finally, sprinkle with coriander leaves.

   Serve as little appetizers with beer or a full-bodied wine.

Good yesterday, better today

*
*
* 10

300 g (10½ oz) tortilla chips

200 g (7 oz) jar of hot salsa

50 g (1¾ oz) chillies

100 g (3½ oz) grated cheese

1 bunch of chives

1

2

Cheese-topped tortilla chips with spicy salsa

From cinema to table

1. Put the tortilla chips in a shallow baking dish and distribute the spicy salsa over them.

2. Slice the chillies and sprinkle evenly over the tortilla chips.

3. Sprinkle with grated cheese – gouda is best. Bake in the oven at 240ºC (475ºF/Gas Mark 9) or place under the grill until the cheese is melted.

Immediately sprinkle with chopped chives and serve straight away.

Good yesterday, better today

✳ ✳ ✳ **15**

■ **You can also top tortilla chips with bolognese sauce, chilli con carne, cheese on its own or avocados.**

3

1 tsp curry powder

1 tsp paprika

1 tsp ground ginger

1 tsp dried marjoram

250 g (9 oz) popped popcorn

1

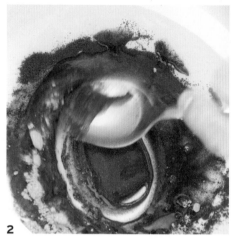

2

Spicy popcorn
Late night show

1. Put the curry powder, paprika and ground ginger in a large bowl along with the dried marjoram and pour on 3 tablespoons of olive oil.

2. Stir the oil and spice mixture.

3. Add the popcorn to the mixture. Ensure the bowl is big enough to mix the popcorn well.

4. Mix the popcorn with the spice mixture.

Enjoy your evening in front of the TV!

Good yesterday, better today

✳
✳
✳
5

■ **Would you like an Indian flavour? Mix 2 teaspoons of tandoori powder with 3 tablespoons of groundnut oil and a little curry powder. Mix with the popcorn as above.**

3

4

1 large potato rösti (Swiss potato pancake)

 **100 g (3¹/₂ oz) pancetta (or thick slices of bacon)**

100 g (3¹/₂ oz) grated cheese

1

2

Cheese-topped rösti with pancetta
Greetings from Switzerland

1. Cut yesterday's rösti pancake into pieces.

2. Cut the pancetta into small strips.

3. Put the pieces of rösti onto a baking tray covered with baking paper and top with strips of pancetta and grated cheese.

4. Sprinkle with plenty of freshly ground black pepper.

5. Bake in the oven at 220°C (425°F/ Gas Mark 7) or under the grill for about 10 minutes until the cheese is melted.

Good yesterday, better today

3

4

5

1/2 pizza

 2 tomatoes

 150 g (5¹/₂ oz) mozzarella cheese

 1 tsp dried oregano

1

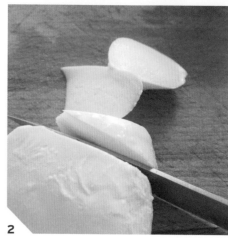
2

Pizza slices baked with tomato and mozzarella
Double-baked pizza

1. Slice the leftover pizza and put it on a baking tray covered with baking paper. Wash and slice the tomatoes.

2. Cut the mozzarella into pieces.

3. Cover the pizza slices with tomato and mozzarella and sprinkle with dried oregano. Finally, drizzle with olive oil.

4. Bake for about 10 minutes in a preheated oven at 220°C (425°F/ Gas Mark 7) or under the grill until the cheese melts.

Good yesterday, better today

20

■ The juicy, fruity flavour of the tomato and mozzarella pieces will revive the leftover pizza.

3

4

1 clove of garlic

 200 ml (7 fl oz) cream

 200 g (7 oz) frozen spinach

 6 frozen fish fingers

 100 g (3$\frac{1}{2}$ oz) grated cheese

1

2

Florentine-style fish fingers on a spinach base
Fish fingers au gratin

1. Peel and roughly chop the clove of garlic. Heat 2 tablespoons of oil in a frying pan and gently fry the garlic until it is transparent.

2. Add the cream and the frozen spinach. Season with salt and pepper.

3. Simmer gently to allow the spinach to break up and mix well into the cream.

4. Fry the fish fingers in a non-stick frying pan in a little oil until golden brown.

5. Spread the cream and spinach mix evenly over the bottom of an oval baking dish. Place the fish fingers on top and sprinkle with the grated cheese. Bake in a preheated oven at 220°C (425°F/ Gas Mark 7) or under the grill for 10 minutes.

Serve in the baking dish. Home-made mashed potatoes will go best with this meal.

Good yesterday, better today

✳
✳✳ 30

■ Place the freshly fried fish fingers on a paper towel to absorb excess oil.

3

4

5

100 g (3¹/₂ oz) canned baby corn

 ¹/₂ bunch of fresh coriander

 1 tsp red curry paste

 400 ml (14 fl oz) coconut milk

300 g (10¹/₂ oz) cooked gnocchi

1

2

Gnocchi in red curry sauce
The day after

1. Drain the baby corn and cut each cob in half once and then again. Wash the coriander and chop coarsely.

2. Heat the curry paste gently in the frying pan with 2 tablespoons of vegetable oil and add the corn cobs.

3. Pour in the coconut milk and bring to the boil.

4. Now add yesterday's cooked gnocchi and simmer gently for 5 minutes.

5. Finally, mix in the chopped coriander.

   Serve in bowls. If desired, garnish with a few chilli flakes.

Good yesterday, better today

* * * 25

■ **Instead of red curry paste, you can use the green or yellow variety. Soya bean sprouts or green asparagus always go well with curry.**

3

4

5

3 tbsp caster sugar

 200 g (7 oz) cooked gnocchi

 250 g (9 oz) ripe strawberries

 100 g (3¹/₂ oz) cottage cheese

1

2

Sweet gnocchi with strawberries

Strawberry ripe

1. In a non-stick frying pan, melt 2 tablespoons of butter with the caster sugar.

2. Add the previous day's cooked gnocchi and fry gently in the sweetened butter.

3. Hull the strawberries. Wash and halve them. Add to the gnocchi.

4. Fry for a further 5 minutes, moving them around the pan, taking care not to let the sugar get too dark.

5. Sprinkle with the cottage cheese and serve immediately.

Good yesterday, better today

■ Quartered apricots or blueberries also turn these simple gnocchi into a surprising pudding.

6 round rice cakes

 2 tbsp strawberry jam

 200 g (7 oz) strawberries

 Peel of 1 orange

1

2

Rice cakes with strawberry jam and strawberries

More strawberries, anyone?

1. Thinly spread the strawberry jam on the rice cakes.

2. Hull the strawberries. Wash the fruit, slice thinly and arrange on the rice cakes.

3. Sprinkle with orange sugar (see below) and then serve as mini fruit tarts.

Good yesterday, better today

 ✳ ✳ ✳ 20

■ Finely mix 4 tablespoons of sugar with orange peel in a blender. Then use this to sprinkle on cakes and puddings.

3

200 g (7 oz) custard

 4 slices of lemon cake

 4 slices of canned pineapple

 8 cocktail cherries

 1 tbsp coconut flakes

1

2

Lemon cake with custard and pineapple

Hawaiian cake

1. Stir the custard with a spoon to make it easier to portion.

2. Arrange the slices of lemon cake on a plate and place 1 tablespoon of custard in the middle of each.

3. Place one slice of pineapple on top of each slice.

4. Finally, decorate with the cocktail cherries and coconut flakes and serve.

   The small cakes in this recipe will serve 4 people.

Good yesterday, better today

■ You can also use nut or orange cake. If you don't have pineapple slices, try canned pears.

3

4

150 g (5¹/₂ oz) plain chocolate

 ¹/₂ tsp cinnamon

 250 g (9 oz) sweet popcorn

1

Popcorn chocolates
Easy as pie chocolates

1. Put the chocolate in a heatproof bowl set over a saucepan of gently simmering water and heat until melted. Add the cinnamon and then stir in 1 tablespoon of oil – this will give the chocolate a glossy appearance.

2. Now add the popcorn to the chocolate and mix carefully.

3. Make little mounds of the chocolate and popcorn mixture and place them on a sheet of baking paper. Set aside for at least 2 hours to allow the chocolate to harden again. Then transfer to bowls or to chocolate boxes.

This is a delicious little treat – home-made chocolates; something that's not so everyday!

Good yesterday, better today

 140

■ Home-made popcorn – put corn kernels into a saucepan with a little oil and heat slowly. When the corn starts to pop, cover the pot. The popcorn will be ready in about 3 minutes.

2

3

about 500 ml (18 fl oz) milk

 1 packet of instant chocolate mousse mix

 6 sponge fingers

 1 very ripe peach

 2 tbsp redcurrant jelly

1

2

Chocolate pudding with sponge fingers and chunks of peach
Peachy chocolate pudding

1. Put the milk in a measuring jug and stir in the instant chocolate mousse mix.

2. Break 4 of the sponge fingers into large pieces and place in two deep bowls or tall glasses.

3. Quarter the ripe peach and peel carefully. Chop into chunks and put on top of the sponge fingers.

4. Spread 1 tablespoon of redcurrant jelly on top of the peach chunks in each glass or bowl.

5. Finally, pour in the thickened chocolate mousse and allow to chill for about 30 minutes in the refrigerator.

Decorate with the remaining sponge fingers.

Good yesterday, better today

✳
✳
✳
45

■ Use a sliced banana instead of the peach, and vanilla instead of the chocolate mousse mixture, and you have a banana split pudding.

3

4

5

1 packet of instant vanilla mousse mix

 about 500 ml (18 fl oz) milk

 1 orange

 6 slices of lemon cake

1

2

Little cakes with vanilla cream and orange slices
Double-orange gateau

1. Put the instant vanilla mousse mix into a bowl and add the cold milk.

2. Stir until smooth with a beater, and then wait until the pudding starts to thicken.

3. Peel the orange with a knife removing the white pith on the orange. Slice the orange.

4. First, put 1 slice of lemon cake on a plate, then put 1 tablespoon of vanilla mousse on top and 1 slice of orange on top of that. Then repeat this process twice.

5. Finish with a pretty slice of orange and your mini gateau is ready.

Good yesterday, better today

 20

■ Drizzle the slices of lemon cake with a little orange liqueur beforehand or spread them with some orange marmalade.

2 slices of any firm cake

 3 tbsp cream cheese

1½ ripe bananas

1

2

Caramelized open banana sandwich with cream cheese
Fireproof bananas

1. Spread the cream cheese onto yesterday's slices of cake.

2. Peel the bananas, halve them once lengthways and then again across, and place on the slices of cake, with the cut surface uppermost.

3. Sprinkle with 2 tablespoons of sugar.

4. Caramelize the sugar with a kitchen blowtorch (you can buy these at kitchen stores).

5. Swing the flame above the sugar (not too close - when the sugar starts to caramelize it can quickly get too dark). As an alternative, you can caramelize the open banana sandwich in a preheated oven at 240°C (475°F/Gas Mark 9) or under the grill.

Incidentally, this is how professional chefs get the crunchy sugar topping on a crème brûlée.

Good yesterday, better today

■ You can use chocolate-hazelnut spread instead of cream cheese, but then use less sugar or your banana sandwich will be too sweet.

420 g (15 oz) canned fruit salad

200 g (7 oz) packet of
marshmallows

1

Fruit salad with marshmallows
Kid's birthday party

1. Drain the fruit salad in a sieve.

2. Then put the fruit salad into a
   baking dish and cover with the
   marshmallows.

3. In a preheated oven at 220°C
   (425°F/Gas Mark 7), bake until
   the marshmallows begin to brown
   (about 10 minutes), or toast under
   the grill.

   Put the dish on the table and
   enjoy!

Good yesterday, better today

 **15**

■ **Try sweet potatoes topped
with toasted marshmallows – a
classic Thanksgiving dinner dish
in the United States.**

2

3

1 ripe apple

 100 g (3^1/$_2$ oz) strawberries

 100 ml (3^1/$_2$ fl oz) apple or orange juice

 4 large scoops of vanilla ice cream

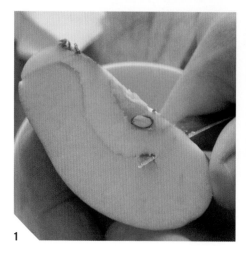

1

2

Hot sugared fruit for pudding
Icy and hot

1. Peel the apple, quarter it and cut out the core.

2. Hull the strawberries, wash and halve them. Cut the apple into chunks.

3. Melt 2 tablespoons of butter and 2 tablespoons of sugar in a frying pan and add the pieces of apple. Gently caramelize for about 3 minutes.

4. Now add the strawberries to the apple chunks. Pour in the juice.

5. Simmer for a further 3–5 minutes until the juice has a sauce-like consistency.

Put 2 scoops of the ice cream into each serving glass. Pour over the hot fruit and serve immediately, before the ice cream melts.

Good yesterday, better today

10 large ice cubes

 500 ml (18 fl oz) milk

 3 tbsp instant cocoa powder

 3 tbsp honey

1

Chocolate and honey sorbet
Cocoa with a spoon

1. Put the ice cubes into a blender and pour the cold milk over them.

2. Sprinkle on the cocoa powder.

3. Add the honey. You can use more if you have a sweet tooth!

4. Now put on the lid and blend, first at medium and then at top speed, until no more ice cubes are visible.

Pour into tall glasses and serve at once. Freshly made chocolate and honey sorbet in only 5 minutes!

Good yesterday, better today

2

3

4

Cooking with leftovers

What's left over after each day...

Almost every time we cook and eat, there are leftovers. They make a wonderful starting point for completely original new meals or for old, almost forgotten dishes.

The priority here is to make the best out of very little. It is to use leftovers creatively, economically, tastily and nutritiously - all for the pure pleasure of eating.

Some of these dishes can be found in three-star restaurants - what more is there to say?

2 slices stale white bread

 1 clove of garlic

 1 ripe tomato

1

2

Tomato bread with olive oil
Hard bread and soft red

1. Toast the white bread in the toaster. Peel the garlic and rub it lightly over the bread.

2. Rub the soft tomato onto the bread.

3. Keep rubbing the tomato until you are left with just the tomato skin in your hand.

4. Drizzle with good olive oil and sprinkle with salt.

   Put some prosciutto on top and garnish with a few olives.

Cooking with leftovers

✳
✳
✳ 5

■ **For an Italian version of this, toast the bread, rub it with garlic, put slices of tomato on top, drizzle with olive oil and scatter with chopped basil.**

300 g (10¹/₂ oz) beef tartare

 1 egg

1

2

Fried beef tartare meatballs with mustard
All or nothing

1. Mix the leftover beef with the egg
    and roll into little balls.

2. Gently fry the meatballs in a frying
    pan coated with 1 tablespoon of
    oil. Handle them very carefully
    while they are cooking.

3. Depending on their size, fry the
    meatballs for 5-8 minutes, lift
    them out carefully with a spatula
    and put onto plates.

Serve with a small dab of
mustard. This is delicious with
some good granary bread.

Cooking with leftovers

■ **This is also good with pork.
Make sure the meatballs are well
cooked through. Don't be afraid
to use yesterday's leftover
mince as well.**

3

4 ripe tomatoes

 1/2 leek

 135 g (4³/₄ oz) canned tuna in oil

 4 black olives

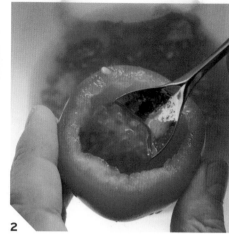

Stuffed tomatoes
The last can of tuna

1. Wash the tomatoes, remove the stalks and cut a slice off the top of each tomato about 2 cm (³/₄ inch) thick. Then use a knife to lift out the flesh in a wedge shape.

2. Use a small spoon to extract a little more of the flesh and set aside.

3. Halve the leek, wash it and slice it finely. Drain the tuna and put it into a bowl with the leek. Add 2 tablespoons of olive oil, season generously with salt and black pepper and mix well.

4. Fill the hollow tomatoes with the tuna salad mix and put the tomato lid back on top.

5. Press the tomato flesh through a fine sieve. Mix the resulting juice with salt, black pepper and a little olive oil and drizzle over the tomatoes like a marinade. Finally, garnish the top of each tomato with an olive.

Cooking with leftovers

3

4

5

100 g (3¹/₂ oz) canned butter beans

 ¹/₂ bunch of parsley

 ¹/₂ tsp paprika

 juice of half a lemon

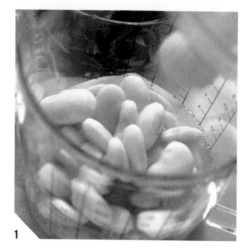
1

2

Butter bean dip with parsley and garlic
Bean dip

1. Pour away half of the liquid from the can and put the beans into a measuring jug.

2. Wash the parsley, shake it dry and pull the leaves off the stalk. Add to the beans.

3. Season with salt and the paprika.

4. Add the lemon juice and 3 tablespoons of olive oil. The simplest way to catch the pips is to squeeze the juice through a sieve.

5. Now use a hand-held stick blender to make a fine purée and put it into a bowl.

   Sprinkle a little paprika on top and garnish with parsley. Serve with pieces of toast cut into strips.

Cooking with leftovers

■ This is also good with scarlet runner beans or red kidney beans. Dress with a little chilli oil and cumin and serve with tortilla chips.

3

4

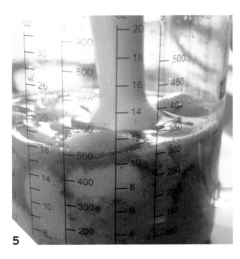

5

2 tbsp mayonnaise

 120 g (4¼ oz) canned sardines in oil

 2 hard-boiled eggs

 1 tsp hot mustard

1

Sardine and egg spread

From the can to the bread

1. Put the mayonnaise into a bowl. Lift the sardines out of the oil with a fork and add them to the bowl.

2. Use a grater to grate the hard-boiled eggs finely and then add to the mixture.

3. Finally, add the mustard. Season with salt and pepper and mix well with a fork.

Spread generously on a piece of toasted bread and sprinkle with a little paprika and chopped green chilli. Delicious with a cold beer!

Cooking with leftovers

10 spring roll wrappers

 200 g (7 oz) fried rice

 1 egg white

2 litres (3¹/₂ pints) oil for frying

1

2

Fried rice spring rolls
Spring rolls with rice

1. Thaw out the spring roll wrappers if necessary, and carefully separate the individual sheets. Only work on 2 sheets at the same time, as they dry out quickly and are then impossible to roll. Put 2 tablespoons of rice into the middle of each one.

2. Brush the outer edges with egg white.

3. Fold the left-hand corner over the rice.

4. Fold the right-hand corner over the rice and brush again with egg white. Then fold the bottom and the top ends over and shape the form into a roll. Continue to make the rest of the spring rolls in this way.

5. Cook for 3–5 minutes in the hot oil until golden.

   Drain briefly on some paper towels and serve in a bowl with a spicy sauce for dipping.

Cooking with leftovers

✳
✳
✳ 30

■ **Instead of fried rice, you could also use savoury meat rice, paella or risotto.**

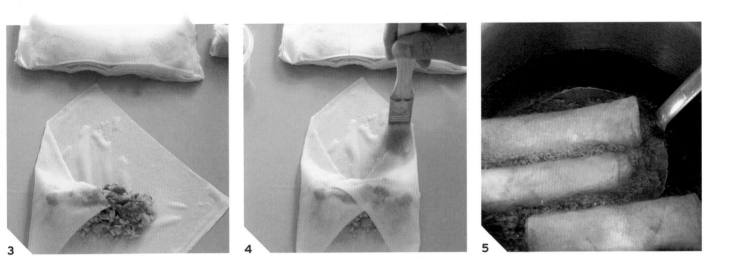

3

4

5

-  200 g (7 oz) vegetable risotto

- 100 g (3½ oz) mince

- 60 g (2¼ oz) grated cheese

- 2 eggs

- 200 g (7 oz) breadcrumbs

- 2 litres (3½ pints) oil for frying

1

2

Pan-fried cheese and rice balls

Rice croquettes

1. Put the risotto, mince and cheese into a bowl.

2. Separate the eggs and add the yolks to the rice mixture. Save the egg whites in a bowl for the coating. Now mix the croquette mixture thoroughly.

3. Form into little balls with your hands.

4. Dip each ball first in the egg white and then in the breadcrumbs.

5. Fry the croquettes in hot oil for 3–5 minutes. Lift them out of the oil with a slotted spoon and drain them on some paper towels.

Put on plates and serve with lemon wedges and a spicy sauce.

Cooking with leftovers

■ You can also use mashed potato instead of rice. Add your favourite extra ingredients and herbs to the mixture.

3   **4**   **5**

1 cooked chicken breast

 1 tomato

 4 slices of bread

 4 tbsp mayonnaise

 2 lettuce leaves

 4 pickled gherkins

 4 tbsp mustard

1

Chicken sandwich with tomato and mustard
Retro chicken

1. Cut the chicken breast into thin slices. Wash the tomato and slice.

2. Toast the bread until golden and spread with mayonnaise.

3. Put a leaf of lettuce and 2 slices of tomato on 2 of the pieces of toast, then put the sliced chicken on top.

4. Slice the pickled gherkins lengthways and put on top of the chicken. Put a generous amount of smooth mustard over the gherkin slices – these sandwiches need to be piquant! Put the remaining slices of toast on top and cut in half diagonally.

Put each sandwich into a paper napkin and use a toothpick to hold the sandwich together. Serve with a cold beer.

Cooking with leftovers

✳
✳   10
✳

■ **Have you more cooked chicken left over? Remove the skin and use the meat for sandwiches.**

2

3

4

½ leek

 2 potatoes boiled in their skins

3 eggs

1 ripe tomato

1

2

Potato and tomato scramble
Good morning, sunshine!

1. Wash the leek well and chop it into thin slices. Peel the leftover potatoes and dice into 2-cm (3/4-inch) chunks.

2. Heat 3 tablespoons of olive oil in a non-stick pan. Add the potatoes and cook for about 2 minutes until they are a light golden colour. Season with salt and pepper and add the chopped leek.

3. Beat the eggs. Wash the tomato and cut it into chunks and add to the egg mixture.

4. Pour the egg and tomato mixture into the pan over the potatoes.

5. Cook the egg mixture until set, stirring all the time, and then put onto plates.

Drizzle with some good olive oil and a generous grind of black pepper.

Cooking with leftovers

✳✳✳ 15

■ Don't have any tomatoes? Then use peppers, courgette, aubergine or red onions.

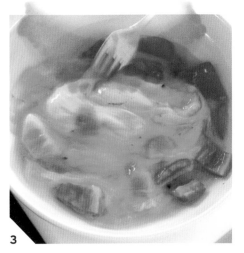

3

4

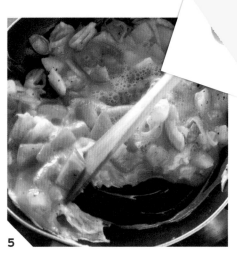

5

500 g (1 lb 2 oz) leftover mashed potato

 100 g (3¹/₂ oz) frozen peas

 2 eggs

 300 g (10¹/₂ oz) breadcrumbs

 2 litres (3¹/₂ pints) oil for frying

1

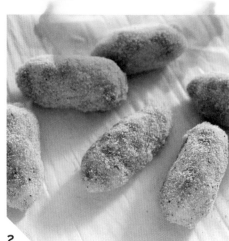
2

Potato croquettes with peas
Mash from the pan

1. Mix the leftover mashed potato with the peas in a bowl. Separate the eggs, adding the egg yolks to the mixture and putting the whites in a bowl to one side for the coating. Mix the potato, peas and egg yolks together with a spoon and then shape into little croquettes.

2. Dip the croquettes into the egg white first and then into the breadcrumbs. Continue this process until the croquettes are well coated in breadcrumbs.

3. Heat the oil in a saucepan and add the croquettes. Cook for about 3 minutes, until golden, and drain on some paper towels.

   Serve on a plate as a little snack, or use to accompany meat or poultry dishes.

Cooking with leftovers

25

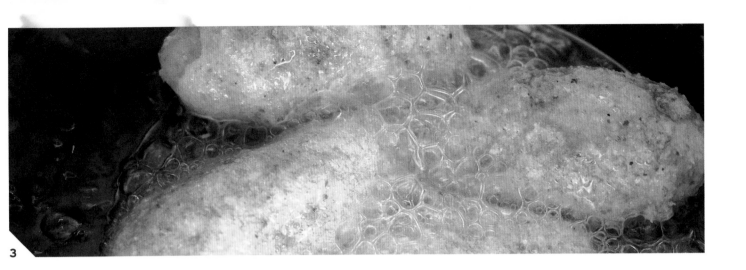

3

 **5 tuna sushi**

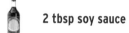 **1 tbsp sesame seeds**

 **1 portion cooked spinach**

2 tbsp soy sauce

1

2

Pan-fried tuna sushi with sesame spinach
Yesterday's sushi, part II

1. Put the sushi onto a plate and lift the pieces of raw tuna off the rice. The green Japanese horseradish sauce - wasabi - will be left on the rice.

2. Put the rice, with the wasabi side up, into a non-stick pan. Put the sesame seeds into the pan to one side of the rice and toast lightly.

3. Now put the spinach on top of the sesame seeds and mix - just watch the rice to make sure it doesn't fall apart.

4. Move the spinach to one side of the pan, turn the rice over and put the tuna slices into the pan.

5. Add the soy sauce to the spinach. Remove the rice from the pan and place on a small serving dish. Top with the sesame spinach, then add the fried tuna.

Here you have a mini fish dish, which used to be sushi!

Cooking with leftovers

* * * 10

■ **For this dish, you could also use sushi made with other fish such as salmon, mackerel, sea bream, catfish or scallops.**

3

4

5

100 g (3^1/$_2$ oz) tempura batter

 2 tbsp hijiki (dried seaweed)

 10 gyoza (dumpling cases)

 2 litres (3^1/$_2$ pints) oil for frying

Filled dumplings fried in tempura and seaweed batter

Underwater cooking

1. Prepare the tempura batter with water according to the directions on the packet.

2. Soak the seaweed in water according to the packet directions, then drain it, add to the batter and stir.

3. Put the dumplings cases into the batter and coat well on all sides.

4. Fry in the hot oil for 3-4 minutes. Then remove and drain on paper towels.

Serve the dumplings with some soy sauce for dipping.

Cooking with leftovers

✳
✳ 30
✳

■ Put the dumplings onto paper towels as soon as they have cooked, in order to soak up any excess oil.

2 spring onions

 100 g (3¹/₂ oz) coarse sausages

 100 g (3¹/₂ oz) pan-fried small
green peppers

2 slices of white bread

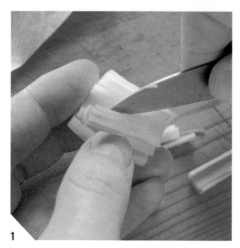
1

2

Mini kebabs with baby green peppers
Spanish kebabs

1. Peel the onions, halve them and cut into pieces. Remove the inner green part. Slice the sausage pieces the same size as the onions'.

2. Thread the pieces of onion, sausage and green pepper onto a small skewer.

3. Put the green pepper kebabs into a frying pan with 2 tablespoons of olive oil and cook on one side for about 3 minutes until golden brown.

4. Turn the kebabs over and cook for a further 3 minutes on the other side.

Toast the slices of white bread, put the cooked kebabs on top and serve.

The juices from the sausage meat will soak into the bread - eat the bread as well or decide to stay slim!

Cooking with leftovers

20

3

4

2-3 bread rolls, depending on size

 6 slices of salami

 1 tomato

 1 large onion

 1 spring onion

1

2

Bread, onion and tomato salad
Salad to go

1. Break the bread into pieces and place in a bowl, cover with 3 tablespoons of white wine vinegar and 5 tablespoons of olive oil and leave to stand for 10 minutes, stirring frequently.

2. Chop up the salami and the tomato.

3. Peel the onion, halve it and cut into slices lengthways.

4. Add all of the chopped ingredients to the bread mixture. Season with salt and pepper.

5. Mix together carefully. Finely chop the spring onions and scatter over the salad before serving.

Cooking with leftovers

✳
✳ **25**
✳

■ **If the bread is too dry, soak it with an additional 2-3 tablespoons of water.**

3

4

5

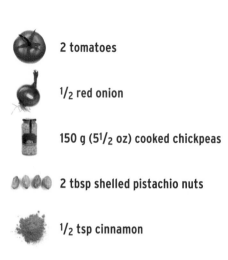

2 tomatoes

½ red onion

150 g (5½ oz) cooked chickpeas

2 tbsp shelled pistachio nuts

½ tsp cinnamon

1

2

Chickpea salad
Oriental summer salad

1. Cut the stalks out of the tomatoes in a wedge shape, then wash the tomatoes and cut into small pieces.

2. Chop the onion finely and put into a bowl with the tomato and the drained chickpeas.

3. Chop the pistachio nuts roughly with a large knife.

4. Add the pistachio nuts and the cinnamon to the chickpea mixture. Season with salt and black pepper.

5. Add 3 tablespoons of olive oil and mix together.

   Taste for seasoning and serve in individual glasses. This is delicious with Turkish sesame seed bread.

Cooking with leftovers

✳
✳
✳ 15

3

4

5

3 cooked potatoes

 3 cooked carrots

 1 piece of cooked celeriac

 2 tbsp mayonnaise

a dash of Worcestershire sauce

1

2

Potato and vegetable salad
Russian salad

1. Chop the potatoes, carrots and celeriac into $1/2$-cm ($1/4$-inch) chunks.

2. Put these into a bowl and add the mayonnaise.

3. Season with black pepper, 4 tablespoons of white wine vinegar and the Worcestershire sauce.

4. Mix all of the ingredients together and season with salt. Ideally you should leave the mixture to marinate for 1 hour if you have time and are not too hungry!

Spoon onto plates and garnish with wedges of hard-boiled eggs and tomato.

Cooking with leftovers

✳
✳
✳ 15
+ 60 min marinating

■ Instead of using carrots and celeriac, you could also use root vegetables from a soup or boiled meat – this tastes particularly good if they have been cooked in a good stock.

3

4

100 g (3¹/₂ oz) tofu

 2 hard-boiled eggs

3 tbsp mayonnaise

1 tsp hot mustard

1

2

Eggs with tofu mayonnaise
Gourmet tofu

1. Grate the tofu finely and put it into a bowl.

2. Cut the hard-boiled eggs in half, lift the yolks out with a spoon and add to the tofu. Carefully rinse the egg whites and leave to dry on a paper towel.

3. Add the mayonnaise, mustard, salt and pepper to the tofu and egg yolk mix.

4. Mix all of the ingredients together with a fork to form a smooth consistency.

5. Fill the egg white halves with the mixture.

Serve the eggs in a dish on a bed of finely chopped lettuce and garnish with capers and a few pieces of finely sliced tomato.

Cooking with leftovers

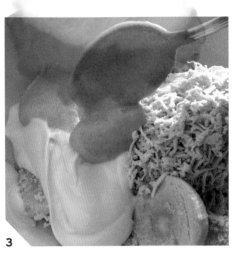

3

4

5

1 leek

 1 red pepper

 160 g (5³/₄ oz) canned sweetcorn

 300 g (10¹/₂ oz) cooked long-grain rice

5 basil leaves

Rice salad
Rice and corn

1. Slice the green part of the leek into thin rings.

2. Wash the red pepper, remove the core, cut into quarters, then slice and finally chop into 1-cm (¹/₂-inch) cubes. Drain the sweetcorn.

3. Add the chopped pepper, chopped leek and the sweetcorn to the rice in a bowl. Slice the basil leaves into strips and put them into the bowl.

4. Dress with 3 tablespoons of white wine vinegar, 2 tablespoons of olive oil, salt and black pepper.

5. Mix everything together well.

Serve the rice salad in a bowl or divide onto plates. This is a perfect salad for a summer party.

Cooking with leftovers

 25

■ If you have any ham, smoked turkey breast, a piece of boiled meat or even some cooked steak left over, simply chop up and add t the salad.

3

4

5

1/2 small cucumber

2 spring onions

250 g (9 oz) cooked couscous

100 g (3 1/2 oz) yogurt –
preferably Greek-style yogurt

juice of 1/2 lemon

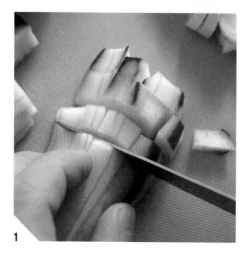
1

2

Couscous salad with yogurt
In the summertime...

1. Peel the cucumber roughly, so that some of the skin is left on. Then cut the cucumber into 1-cm (1/2-inch) pieces.

2. Chop the spring onions into rings and put into a bowl with the couscous and the cucumber.

3. Add the yogurt and season with salt and black pepper.

4. Remove the pips from the lemon half and then squeeze the juice over the salad.

5. Finally, add 2 tablespoons of olive oil to the couscous salad and mix everything together carefully.

Spoon onto plates and garnish with pieces of lemon and fresh mint.

Cooking with leftovers

20

3

4

5

3 spring onions

400 g (14 oz) potatoes boiled in their skins

2 tbsp mayonnaise

1 tbsp pesto

1

Potato salad with pesto
Just stirred - not puréed

1. Wash the spring onions, cut off the green ends and the roots and slice the white part into thin rings.

2. Peel the leftover cooked potatoes and slice them directly into a bowl with the spring onions.

3. Season with salt and pepper. Add the mayonnaise and the pesto.

4. Mix together carefully using 2 large spoons and divide up onto plates.

Garnish with a few lettuce leaves and, if you want to be even more Italian, spoon a little more pesto over the top.

Cooking with leftovers

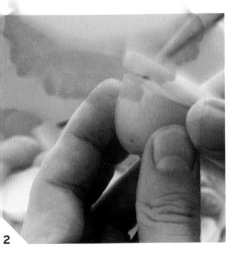

2

3

4

1 thumb-sized piece of ginger

 200 g (7 oz) cauliflower florets

 150 g (5¼ oz) canned peeled tomatoes

 300 g (10½ oz) lentils from a jar

 750 ml (1¼ pints) vegetable stock

1

2

Quick lentil and vegetable soup
First stirred, then puréed

1. Peel the ginger and grate it finely.

2. Cut the cauliflower into slices. Sweat the cauliflower and the grated ginger in 2 tablespoons of butter. Season with salt and pepper and add the tomatoes.

3. Add the lentils and stir well.

4. Pour over the stock and simmer for 10 minutes, stirring occasionally.

5. Purée the soup with a hand-held stick blender and taste for seasoning.

   Serve in bowls and garnish with a blob of soured cream or crème fraîche.

Cooking with leftovers

* * * 30

■ Pour the broth into the lentil jar. Put the lid on and shake – this way you will get the last of the lentils into the soup instead of leaving them behind in the jar.

3

4

5

3 cloves of garlic

100 g (3¹/₂ oz) very ripe tomatoes or cherry tomatoes

750 ml (1¹/₂ pints) water or vegetable stock

1

2

Garlic and tomato soup
Poor man's garlic soup

1. Peel the garlic cloves, slice them thinly and then, using a large knife, chop them very finely with ¹/₂ teaspoon of salt.

2. Remove the stalks from the tomatoes, wash and cut them into quarters.

3. Melt 2 tablespoons of butter in a saucepan and add in the garlic and chopped tomatoes.

4. Sweat the tomatoes and the garlic until they become soft. Then season with salt and black pepper.

5. Pour over the water or the stock and simmer for 5 minutes.

Serve in warmed soup bowls. Wholemeal bread or croutons are good with this – and you have a simple but absolutely delicious soup meal ready!

Cooking with leftovers

25

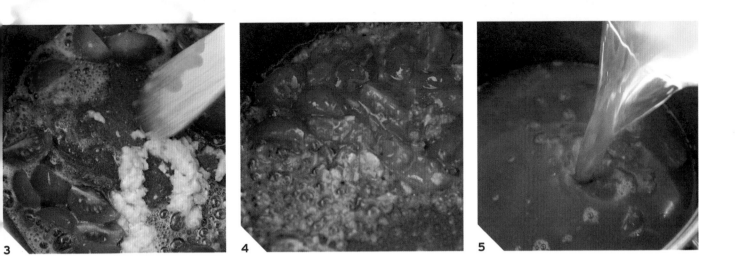

 500 ml (18 fl oz) tomato juice

1 red onion

1 bunch of thyme

zest of 1 lemon

1

2

Quick tomato soup
Tomato juice ready for the spoon

1. Put the tomato juice into a blender.

2. Add salt, black pepper and 3 tablespoons of good olive oil.

3. Peel the onion and cut one half in chunks and the other in rings. Pull the leaves off the thyme and add to the tomato juice with the onion chunks. Set aside the onion rings for later.

4. Cut the lemon zest into fine strips and add to the tomato juice. Close the lid tightly and purée well on the middle setting.

5. Pour the tomato soup into a saucepan and bring to a boil. Add more salt and pepper if needed.

   Ladle into soup bowls, sprinkle a few onion rings over the soup and serve.

Cooking with leftovers

 20

1 cooked chicken breast

 1/2 red pepper

 1 lime

 600 ml (1 pint) coconut milk

 1 tsp miso (sweet-sour soup paste)

1

2

Coconut milk and chicken soup
Who's taken the coconut?

1. Slice up the chicken breast, cut the red pepper into quarters, core it and cut into strips. Chop the lime into pieces.

2. Put the coconut milk into a saucepan and bring slowly to the boil.

3. First add in the chopped lime.

4. Then add the chopped pepper and the chicken pieces and bring to the boil.

5. Now add the miso to the pot and stir. Simmer gently for about 3 minutes until the pieces of pepper are cooked.

Serve in soup bowls. If you have any fresh coriander leaves, sprinkle them over the soup.

Cooking with leftovers

25

■ Bring to the boil 1 part coconut flakes and 2 parts water and then sieve through a cloth. This will give you some wonderful home-made coconut milk!

 750 ml (1¹/₂ pints) milk

4-6 cooked potatoes

1 pinch of nutmeg

1 tsp dried marjoram

1

2

3

Potato soup

Express soup from the blender

1. Put the milk into a blender.

2. Add 4-6 potatoes.

3. ... or more if they are small.

4. Add the nutmeg, salt, black pepper and dried marjoram. Put the lid on the blender.

5. Blend at the highest setting until the potatoes are finely puréed and the soup has a nice creamy consistency.

6. Transfer the mixture to a saucepan and simply heat through. Season with a little more salt, if needed.

Scatter freshly baked croutons over the soup and serve.

Cooking with leftovers

 ✳
✳
✳ 15

1 litre (1³/₄ pints) beef stock

 1 pinch of nutmeg

 2 slices of stale bread

 2 eggs

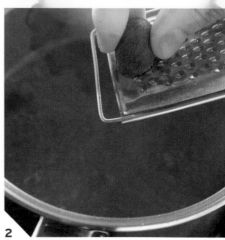

Beef and egg broth
Just not foamy!

1. Put the beef stock into a saucepan and bring to the boil (see tip below).

2. Season with the pinch of nutmeg.

3. Cut the stale bread into chunks and sauté in a frying pan with 2 tablespoons of hot olive oil until crispy.

4. Now beat the eggs.

5. Pour the beaten eggs into the soup and bring back up to the boil.

Pour into soup bowls and serve with the croutons on top.

Cooking with leftovers

■ Generally, fresh beef stock keeps in the refrigerator for about 5 days. If it begins to foam, it's no longer okay to use.

100 g (3½ oz) soft butter

 3 egg yolks

 1 pinch of nutmeg

 100 g (3½ oz) spinach leaves (either frozen or left over)

 125 g (4½ oz) breadcrumbs

 10 sage leaves

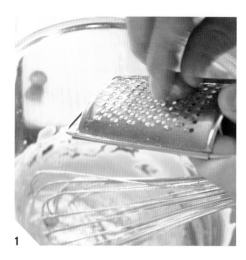

1

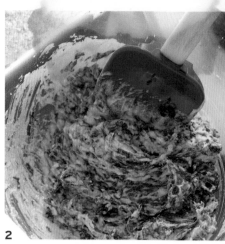

2

Bread and spinach gnocchi

Breadcrumbs Italia

1. Beat the butter in a bowl until it is creamy and then add the egg yolks and mix well. Season with salt, freshly ground black pepper and the nutmeg.

2. Chop the spinach roughly and add it to the butter along with the breadcrumbs. Mix well.

3. Let the batter rest for about 10 minutes and then make into little gnocchi shapes using 2 teaspoons.

4. Put the gnocchi on a plate in the refrigerator and leave to chill for 20 minutes – this way they will keep their shape better.

5. Bring some lightly salted water to the boil in a saucepan and drop in the cold gnocchi. Bring back to the boil, cover, and simmer for about 20 minutes. Meanwhile, melt 3 tablespoons of butter in a frying pan and, when it starts to foam, add the roughly chopped sage leaves and sauté until they are crisp.

   Put the gnocchi on a plate and pour over the sage butter.

Cooking with leftovers

✳
✳ **60**
✳

■ **The sage leaves must be nice and crispy in order to flavour the butter. You could also use rosemary instead of sage.**

3

4

5

1 tbsp smooth mustard

 1 onion

 3 cooked bread dumplings

 1 bunch of chives

1

2

Dumpling salad
Super fresh

1. Put the mustard with a pinch each of salt, black pepper and sugar into a bowl.

2. Add 3 tablespoons of red wine vinegar and mix well.

3. Beat 5 tablespoons of vegetable oil into the marinade until smooth.

4. Peel the onion and chop it finely. Chop the dumplings into pieces approximately (5 mm) 1/4 inch thick and add to the marinade along with the onion.

5. Mix together carefully.

   Chop the chives roughly, scatter on top and serve.

Cooking with leftovers

✳
✳
✳ 15

3

4

5

½ aubergine

 1 courgette

 1 green pepper

2 onions

150 g (5½ oz) canned peeled tomatoes

1

2

Pan-fried vegetables
Instant ratatouille

1. Cut the aubergine into long strips and then into chunks.

2. Wash the courgette and the green pepper, deseed and chop into chunks. Peel the onions and chop them finely.

3. Heat 4 tablespoons of olive oil in a wide saucepan, add the aubergine and sweat for about 5 minutes.

4. Then add the courgette and the green pepper. Season with salt and black pepper and cook for a further 5 minutes.

5. Drain the tomatoes well, add to the saucepan and stir. Cook for about 20 minutes, stirring frequently. The pan-fried vegetables are ready when the juice of the tomatoes has almost completely evaporated.

Garnish with fresh basil leaves.

Cooking with leftovers

✳
✳
✳ 40

500 g (1 lb 2 oz) potatoes boiled in their skins

 1 red onion

1

2

Sautéed potatoes with red onion
For amateur cooks

1. Peel the potatoes. Heat 2 tablespoons of vegetable oil in a non-stick pan and slice the potatoes directly into the pan.

2. Season well with salt and black pepper.

3. Sauté gently for about 10 minutes, tossing or stirring frequently – depending on your ability!

4. Peel the onion and use a grater to grate it directly over the potatoes.

5. Continue to sauté for a further 5 minutes and then spoon onto plates.

This is very good with cooked ham, herring fillets, meat loaf, meatballs or a fried egg with creamed spinach.

Cooking with leftovers

400 g (14 oz) mashed potato

 50 g (1³/₄ oz) soured cream

2 tbsp snipped chives

 3 eggs

100 g (3¹/₂ oz) spinach leaves

1

2

Potato pancakes
Just like Mother made

1. Put the leftover mashed potato into a bowl with the soured cream and the chives.

2. Mix well with a wooden spoon, until there are no lumps left.

3. Add in one of the eggs and beat well.

4. Heat 1 tablespoon of vegetable oil in a non-stick frying pan. Spoon heaped tablespoonfuls of the batter into to the pan and cook for a few minutes on each side, until browned.

Break the remaining eggs into the frying pan and fry them in a little butter. Toss the spinach in some butter, then put it on top of the pancakes and top each one with a fried egg.

Cooking with leftovers

30

■ **If the potato pancakes break up in the frying pan when you are turning them, you can still serve them as mini-pancakes!**

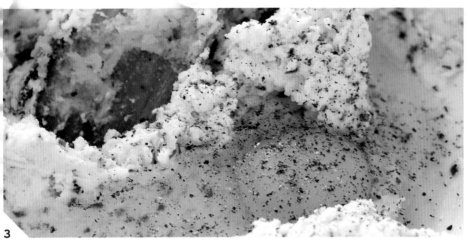

1 onion

 300 g (10$^{1}/_{2}$ oz) cooked pasta
(penne or ribbon noodles)

 100 g (3$^{1}/_{2}$ oz) smoked bacon or
cooked ham

 1 pinch of nutmeg

 2 eggs

1

2

Pasta with bacon
A classic

1. Peel the onion and cut into slices. Melt 2 tablespoons of butter in a frying pan and when it starts to foam, add the sliced onion and cook until it is transparent.

2. Add the pasta to the pan and cook for a further 3 minutes.

3. Slice the bacon thinly and add to the pan. Season with salt and black pepper. Sprinkle the nutmeg over the contents of the pan.

4. Beat the eggs in a deep bowl and season with salt and black pepper.

5. Pour the eggs over the pasta and stir constantly until the eggs thicken.

Serve!

Cooking with leftovers

3

4

5

1½ tsp dried ginger

 1½ tsp curry powder

 500 g (1 lb 2 oz) cooked pasta

 100 ml (3½ fl oz) tomato ketchup

 100 g (3½ oz) grated cheese

1 tbsp chopped parsley

1

Curry pasta with ketchup
It doesn't get any simpler...

1. Heat the ginger and the curry powder in 1 tablespoon of melted butter in a saucepan.

2. Add the cooked pasta and stir.

3. Squirt the ketchup straight from the bottle over the pasta.

4. Sprinkle with the grated cheese and the chopped parsley.

5. Stir until the cheese has melted. Season with salt and black pepper.

Cooking with leftovers

✳
✳
✳ 10

■ With a good dash of Tabasco sauce, this makes especially good hangover food. For this reason, always keep some cooked pasta in the refrigerator!

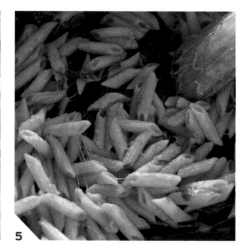

3   **4**   **5**

1 red onion

 400 g (14 oz) mince

 150 g (5^1/$_2$ oz) jarred chilli sauce

 380 g (13^1/$_4$ oz) canned baked beans in tomato sauce

 160 g (5^3/$_4$ oz) canned sweetcorn

1

2

Chilli con carne
Chilli con carne for beginners

1. Chop the onion into pieces. Heat 3 tablespoons of oil in a saucepan and fry the onion. Add the mince and fry until it's browned.

2. Add the chilli sauce to the meat. Use a good spicy sauce as this will give the right flavour.

3. Add 1 cup of water and simmer for 30 minutes.

4. Add the baked beans and the sweetcorn. Bring to a simmer again.

Serve in deep bowls. Garnish with a blob of soured cream and a dash of Tabasco sauce. Don't forget to serve some bread with the chilli con carne, in case it's too spicy.

Cooking with leftovers

✳
✳ 45
✳

3

4

1 ready-rolled pizza base

 250 g (9 oz) chilli con carne

 10 cherry tomatoes

 3 tbsp grated cheese

1

Chilli con carne pizza
Advanced chilli con carne

1. Put the pizza base on a baking tray lined with baking paper and then spread the chilli con carne over the pizza base. Be sure to leave about 3 cm (1 1/4 inch) around the edges free of sauce.

2. Halve the cherry tomatoes and scatter them on top of the sauce.

3. Finally, sprinkle the grated cheese on top. Preheat the oven to 220°C (425°F/Gas Mark 7), put the pizza in and bake for about 20 minutes until crispy.

Take the pizza out of the oven, cut into slices and serve on a plate or a wooden board.

Cooking with leftovers

* * * 30

■ You can put anything on this pizza that goes with chilli, for example jalapeños, chilli beans or red chillies.

2

3

3 potatoes

 300 g (10¹/₂ oz) bolognese sauce

 100 g (3¹/₂ oz) soured cream

 100 g (3¹/₂ oz) grated cheese

 1 medium aubergine

Potato gratin with soured cream and aubergine
Warning - this is addictive!

1. Peel the potatoes and cut into slices about 5 mm (¹/₄ inch) thick. Brush a baking dish with 1 tablespoon of olive oil and then cover the base with a layer of potato. Then spread half the bolognese sauce over the potatoes.

2. Now put half of the soured cream and half of the grated cheese on top to form another layer.

3. Slice the aubergine into pieces 1 cm (¹/₂ inch) thick and add a layer to the dish.

4. Put the remaining bolognese sauce on top and then another layer of potatoes.

5. Finally, put the remaining soured cream and the grated cheese on top. Drizzle a little olive oil over the top. Cover with foil. Preheat the oven to 180°C (350°F/Gas Mark 4) and put the dish in the oven. Bake for 1 hour. 10 minutes before the cooking time is up, remove the foil so that the top goes golden brown.

Bring the dish to the table and serve directly.

Cooking with leftovers

- Before serving, test with a wooden skewer or a fork to see if the potatoes are cooked through.

3

4

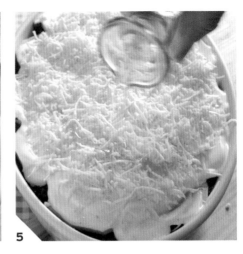

5

 250 g (9 oz) minced beef

1 carrot

1 onion

3 tbsp canned sweetcorn

3 tbsp soy sauce

1

2

Minced beef with soy sauce
You won't get faster than this...

1. Heat 2 tablespoons of vegetable oil in a non-stick frying pan and add the minced beef. Use a wooden spoon to stir the beef.

2. Pan-fry the meat gently until it is browned. If some liquid comes out of the beef, push the meat to one side. This way, the meat juices boil off quicker and the meat acquires a better flavour during cooking.

3. Peel the carrot and the onion, slice and add to the meat. Season with black pepper and continue cooking for a further 5 minutes.

4. Add the sweetcorn to the pan and then the soy sauce. Stir and remove from the heat. If you use soy sauce, you don't need to use salt and the meat takes on a slightly Asian flavour.

Spoon onto plates with mashed potato and sprinkle with some celery leaves.

Cooking with leftovers

 35

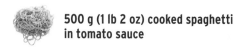 **500 g (1 lb 2 oz) cooked spaghetti in tomato sauce**

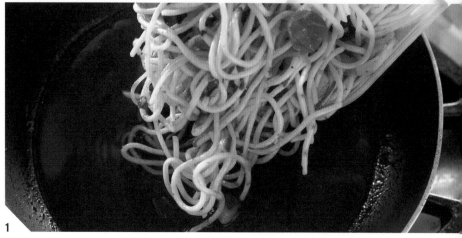

1

Pasta pizza

Yesterday's spaghetti, today's pizza

1. Put the cold spaghetti and tomato sauce (preferably spicy seasoned pasta) into a non-stick frying pan with 4 tablespoons of olive oil. Pan-fry gently!

2. Use a spoon to shape the spaghetti evenly into a round pizza. Continue to pan-fry until the pasta is nice and crispy on one side.

3. Turn the pizza over. Cook for a further 10 minutes until the other side is crispy.

Put the pizza on a plate and divide into four.

Cooking with leftovers

❋
❋ 25
❋

■ Serve with a crisp green salad. You could also put salami and cheese on top of the pizza and then brown it quickly in the oven.

750 ml (1½ pints) tomato juice

6–8 dried lasagne sheets

300 g (10½ oz) paella

100 g (3½ oz) grated cheese

1

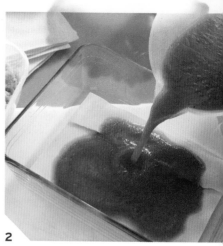
2

Paella lasagne
Paella today, lasagne tomorrow

1. Season the tomato juice well with salt and black pepper and add 3 tablespoons of olive oil to it.

2. Pour some of the tomato juice into a small baking dish, so that the bottom is well covered. Then put a layer of the dried lasagne sheets on top and cover again with tomato juice.

3. Put a layer of the leftover paella on top of the lasagne.

4. Sprinkle the paella layer with grated cheese.

5. Now put on another layer of dried lasagne sheets and cover with tomato juice. Top with more paella and cheese and finish off with a final layer of lasagne topped with grated cheese.

Preheat the oven to 160°C (325°F/ Gas Mark 3), cover with foil and bake for 50 minutes. 10 minutes before the cooking time is up, remove the foil so that the cheese topping goes golden brown.

Serve at the table straight from the baking dish.

Cooking with leftovers

70

■ If the lasagne sheets don't fit in the baking dish, you can break them down to the right size over the edge of a cutting board.

3

4

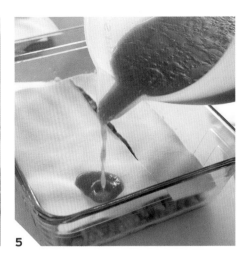

5

 2 large onions

 200 g (7 oz) roast beef

200 g (7 oz) frozen peas

1 tsp paprika

300 g (10½ oz) cooked rice

1

2

Rice with meat and peas
Rice in a second

1. Peel the onions, chop them and cook them in a tablespoon of melted butter in a frying pan.

2. Cut the meat into strips and add to the onions.

3. Pour the peas straight from the packet into the pan and season with the paprika.

4. Continue to pan-fry until the peas are cooked and then season with salt and black pepper.

5. Add the cooked rice and pour in a little water. When the water comes to the boil it will heat the rice through in seconds.

Serve on plates or in bowls and sprinkle with a little hot paprika.

Cooking with leftovers

■ Instead of frozen peas you could use a can of carrots and peas, although frozen vegetables do taste better than canned varieties – with the exception of sauerkraut and red cabbage.

	150 g (5¼ oz) cooked long-grain rice
	200 g (7 oz) mince
	1 onion
	1 egg
	1 tbsp sweet paprika
	2 tbsp mustard

Rice croquettes
Long-grain meatballs

1. Put the rice and the meat into a bowl. Chop the onion and add to the bowl. Add the egg and sweet paprika. Season with salt and pepper and add the mustard.

2. Mix well.

3. Use your hands to form the mixture into sausage shapes, each about 10 cm (4 inches) long.

4. Heat 2 tablespoons of oil in a non-stick frying pan and cook the sausages for 5 minutes on each side.

   Serve on a plate with some chopped onion, hot mustard and gherkins, and some bread or bread rolls.

Cooking with leftovers

✳
✳ 30
✳

■ **When you are making the sausages, wet your hands in lukewarm water so the mince doesn't stick to them.**

3

4

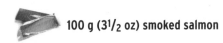 100 g (3¹/₂ oz) smoked salmon

5 basil leaves

4 eggs

1 pinch of nutmeg

1

2

Smoked salmon omelette soufflé
Scrumptious salmon

1. Cut the salmon into strips. Chop the basil leaves finely and set aside with the salmon.

2. Put the eggs into a bowl and grate in some nutmeg.

3. Beat the eggs until they are foamy. Add the salmon and the chopped basil. Season carefully with salt, as the salmon already has quite a strong flavour.

4. Melt 2 tablespoons of butter in an ovenproof non-stick pan and add the egg mixture.

5. Preheat the oven to 220°C (425°F/Gas Mark 7) and cook for about 10 minutes until golden brown.

   Serve immediately.

Cooking with leftovers

✳
✳
✳ 25

■ **Snip the brown bits off the smoked salmon.**

2 ripe tomatoes

1 onion

250 g (9 oz) cooked pasta

100 g (3^1/$_2$ oz) small black olives

100 g (3^1/$_2$ oz) capers

1

2

Italian pasta salad
Italian pasta with a difference

1. Wash the tomatoes and chop into chunks. Peel the onion and chop roughly.

2. Put the chopped tomato, chopped onion, pasta and olives into a bowl.

3. Add the capers to the pasta with a little vinegar. Mix in 3 tablespoons of olive oil and season with salt and black pepper.

4. Toss the salad, garnish with herbs and some more black pepper.

Cooking with leftovers

8

■ **Instead of using vinegar, you could use some liquid from the caper jar.**

3

4

100 g (3¹/₂ oz) butter

 2 eggs

 2 tbsp plain flour

 300 g (10¹/₂ oz) cooked round-grain rice

 100 g (3¹/₂ oz) strawberries

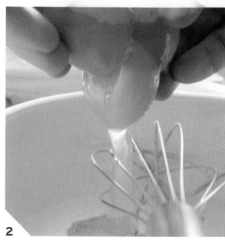

1

2

Rice pudding with strawberries
Deluxe rice pudding

1. Set aside 1 teaspoon of the butter to grease a baking dish. Put the rest of the butter in a bowl, add 3 tablespoons of sugar and beat until creamy.

2. Add the eggs one at a time and beat well. The eggs should be the same temperature as the butter, or the mixture won't be smooth. Now add the flour.

3. Stir the contents of the bowl thoroughly to make sure no little lumps remain.

4. Add in the cold rice gradually and stir well.

5. Grease the baking dish with butter and sprinkle with sugar. Pour the batter from the bowl into the dish and put the hulled strawberries on top. Preheat the oven to 200°C (400°F/Gas Mark 6) and bake for about 35 minutes until golden brown.

Remove from the oven, sprinkle with caster sugar and serve immediately.

Cooking with leftovers

* * * 50

■ Apricots, blueberries or raspberries would also be very good with this dish instead of strawberries.

3   **4**   **5**

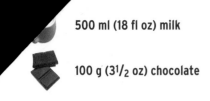

500 ml (18 fl oz) milk

100 g (3½ oz) chocolate

1

2

Piped chocolate cream
Light chocolate mousse

1. Put the milk and the chocolate (white, milk or dark, whichever you like best) into a small saucepan and simmer slowly until the chocolate melts into the milk.

2. Add about 3 tablespoons of sugar to the chocolate, mix, remove from the heat and leave to cool to room temperature.

3. Put the chocolate mix into a piping bag and close it. Leave it in the refrigerator for 1 hour.

4. Attach the filling tip to the piping bag and then pipe the chilled cream into glasses and serve. This is an easy and especially light version of chocolate mousse, as it doesn't have any cream in it.

Cooking with leftovers

✳ ✳ ✳ 90

■ If you don't have a piping bag, beat the well-chilled chocolate mixture with a hand whisk until it is foamy.

3

4

3 apples

 500 g (1 lb 2 oz) dry white bread

 2 eggs

 200 ml (7 fl oz) milk

 50 g (1³/₄ oz) flaked almonds

 1 tsp cinnamon

1

2

Bread pudding with apples and cinnamon
Smells just like Christmas

1. Grease a baking dish with butter and sprinkle with 2 tablespoons of sugar.

2. Peel the apples, quarter them, core them and then cut them lengthways into thin slices. Cut the crusts off the bread and slice it diagonally.

3. Lay the bread triangles and the apple slices in alternate layers in the baking dish. Beat the eggs with the milk and 3 tablespoons of sugar and then pour evenly over the bread and apple slices.

4. Sprinkle with the flaked almonds and another tablespoon of sugar. Finally, dust the top with cinnamon according to taste.

5. Preheat the oven to 180°C (350°F/Gas Mark 4) and bake for 30 minutes.

Dredge with caster sugar and serve. This goes very well with custard or vanilla-flavoured cream.

Cooking with leftovers

50

■ **Put the bread crusts to one side to dry out. Then, later, grate them finely and use as breadcrumbs.**

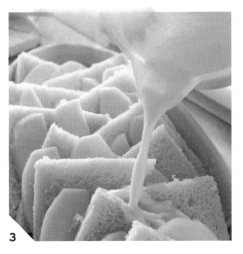

3

4

5

6 slices of stale white bread

 300 ml (10 fl oz) milk

 3 eggs

1

2

Poor man's French toast
Also for rich people...

1. Slice the stale bread diagonally, pour over the cold milk and leave to soak. Then turn the bread over.

2. Add a pinch of salt to the eggs and beat well. Then dip the well-soaked bread slices into the egg mix.

3. Heat 2 tablespoons of butter in a pan until the butter foams and then add the bread slices.

4. Cook the French toast until golden brown on both sides.

   Drain the toast on some paper towels, then put onto plates and sprinkle with cinnamon sugar.

Cooking with leftovers

✳
✳
✳ 15

- To make the cinnamon sugar mix 2 parts granulated sugar with 1 part ground cinnamon.

5 eggs

  150 g (5^1/$_2$ oz) yogurt

 150 g (5^1/$_2$ oz) plain flour

^{1}/$_2$ tsp baking powder

150 g (5^1/$_2$ oz) unsweetened cocoa powder

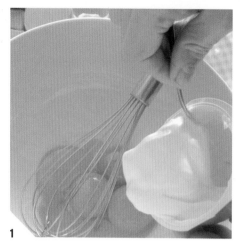

1

2

Moist chocolate yogurt cake
Yogurt pot cake

1. Separate the eggs and put the yolks into a bowl. Add the yogurt. Put the egg whites aside for now in the refrigerator.

2. Rinse out the yogurt pot. You can use this as a measuring cup for the rest of the ingredients. Add 1 pot of sugar to the egg yolks and yogurt and beat together well with a whisk.

3. Add in the flour and the baking powder. Mix well and then add the unsweetened cocoa powder along with a pot of vegetable oil. Stir until smooth.

4. Add a pinch of salt to the egg whites and beat until stiff, then add to the batter and fold in gently.

5. Pour the batter into a 26-cm (10-inch) cake tin. Preheat the oven to 180°C (350°F/Gas Mark 4) and bake for about 50 minutes.

   Test to see if it is cooked with a wooden skewer – insert the skewer into the cake and if it comes out with no cake mix on it, then your cake is ready. This cake makes enough for 4 people.

Cooking with leftovers

* * * 70

■ **You are bound to have a little bit of leftover chocolate in a cupboard or a drawer somewhere – grate it finely and sprinkle over the cake.**

150 g (5½ oz) plain flour

300 ml (10 fl oz) milk

2 tbsp quark (curd cheese)

2 eggs

1 banana

1

2

Banana and quark pancakes
Fit for a king

1. Put the flour into a mixing bowl. Add the milk gradually and beat until the batter is smooth. Add the quark and 3 tablespoons of sugar and mix well. Beat the eggs in last of all, so that the batter stays lighter.

2. Peel the banana and slice it thinly. Mix it carefully into the batter.

3. Heat 1 tablespoon of oil in a non-stick frying pan and pour in the batter. Cook over a gentle heat until golden brown.

4. Cut the pancake into quarters with a wooden spatula and then turn each quarter over to the other side.

5. Continue cooking until the pancake is golden brown on the other side. Then, using 2 wooden spoons, break the pancake into small pieces and sprinkle with a tablespoon of sugar. Continue cooking until the sugar is slightly caramelized.

Dust generously with caster sugar and put onto plates. Sprinkle with some coarsely chopped walnuts and serve.

Cooking with leftovers

✳ ✳ ✳ 20

■ Run a tablespoon of butter around the edge of the frying pan, so the butter melts and runs in under the batter. This way, no bits of pancake get left behind!

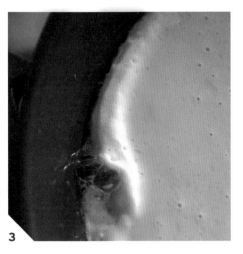

3

4

5

50 g (1³/₄ oz) unsweetened cocoa powder

 200 g (7 oz) cooked pasta (penne or farfalle)

 200 ml (7 fl oz) cream

1

2

Chocolate pasta
Choco pasta

1. Melt 1 tablespoon of butter in a saucepan, add the unsweetened cocoa and stir.

2. Sprinkle 3 tablespoons of sugar over the cocoa.

3. Add the pasta to the saucepan and stir.

4. Pour the cream over the pasta and stir to make a creamy chocolate sauce. Leave to simmer for about 1 minute.

5. The pasta is ready when the sauce sticks to it. Now take it off the heat.

Divide onto plates, put some vanilla ice cream on top and sprinkle with some grated chocolate before serving.

Cooking with leftovers

✳
✳
✳ 10

■ To get pretty chocolate shavings, peel a slab of refrigerated chocolate with a vegetable peeler. Work quickly so the chocolate doesn't melt in your hands.

3

4

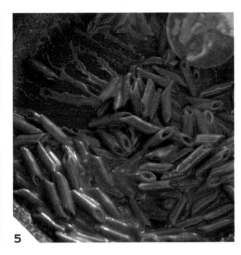

5

3 ripe peaches

 1 tsp cinnamon

 300 g (10¹/₂ oz) cooked long-grain rice

3 tbsp puffed rice

1

2

Sweet peach rice
With a handful of rice

1. Cut the peaches in half, remove the stones and slice into pieces. Put the pieces of peach in a saucepan with 1 tablespoon of butter and sprinkle with 2 tablespoons of sugar.

2. Sprinkle with the cinnamon and mix together well.

3. Cook until the peaches are nice and glossy. When the sugar is thoroughly dissolved into the butter and peach juices, little bubbles of air will form.

4. Now add in the cooked rice.

5. Finally, mix in the puffed rice. This makes the rice a little crispy and gives the dish that extra something.

Cooking with leftovers

✳
✳ 20
✳

■ **This is best made with long-grain rice or savoury basmati rice. Instead of peaches, you can make it with apples, pears, apricots or bananas. Whichever fruit you use, it must be very ripe.**

3

4

5

6-8 stale croissants

 300 g (10^1/$_2$ oz) canned peaches

 500 ml (18 fl oz) milk

 3 eggs

1

2

Croissant pudding with peaches
Fruit brunch

1. Halve the croissants and put them into a baking dish in layers. Cut the peaches into pieces and spread out over the croissants.

2. Put the milk, eggs and 4 tablespoons of sugar into a jug and beat with an electric mixer.

3. Pour the milk and egg mix slowly and evenly over the croissants, so that they soak up the liquid. Leave to stand for about 5 minutes, pressing the croissants into the milk every so often.

4. Sprinkle with 2 tablespoons of sugar, which will caramelize lightly when baking.

5. Preheat the oven to 190°C (375°F/Gas Mark 5) and bake for 25 minutes. The pudding is ready when it has risen by about a third.

Dust the top with icing sugar. Spoon onto plates and pour over some of the peach juice from the can. This pudding serves 4 people.

Cooking with leftovers

3

4

5

Favourite foods with a difference

New discoveries

You might well have eaten potato pancakes but what about potato pancakes without potatoes? Or potato crisps turned into a tortilla? How about cornflakes in scrambled egg? Or salmon burgers?

Just do things differently once in a while – that's what these recipes are all about. The results are surprisingly tasty, and very easy to make.

And by the way, there are incredible numbers of combinations still waiting for you to discover. Why not write your own cookbook?

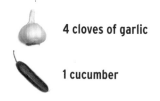

4 cloves of garlic

1 cucumber

1

2

Oil-free cucumber salad
Made for diets

1. Peel the garlic, chop it finely and sprinkle it with a pinch of salt.

2. Crush the garlic and the salt with the back of a knife.

3. Peel the cucumber in strips, halve it, remove the seeds and grate roughly into the garlic mix.

4. Season with 2 tablespoons of white wine vinegar, a pinch of salt, 1 tablespoon of sugar and freshly ground black pepper. Leave to marinate in the refrigerator for 30 minutes.

This goes well with fried chicken breasts.

Favourite foods with a difference

40

3

4

250 g (9 oz) canned sweetcorn

1 egg

 1 tbsp plain flour

1

2

Sweetcorn pancakes with tomato salsa

No-potato potato pancakes

1. Drain the canned sweetcorn well and squeeze out some of the moisture, then put it in a food processor. Add the egg and flour and season with salt and black pepper.

2. Close the lid of the blender and blend thoroughly.

3. Heat 1 tablespoon of oil in a non-stick frying pan, spoon in the mixture with a tablespoon and shape little pancakes.

4. Fry the pancakes gently and turn carefully with a spatula after about 3 minutes.

5. Leave to drain on paper towels. Take care when handling them, as these pancakes will be very loose and will easily fall apart.

   Serve on plates with tomato salsa and leaves of parsley.

Favourite foods with a difference

- For the tomato salsa, cut a tomato into small pieces. Season with salt and pepper, mix with 1 tablespoon of yogurt and 1 tablespoon of olive oil, and add a few splashes of chilli sauce to give the salsa some zing.

1 onion

 4 eggs

 200 g (7 oz) potato crisps

1

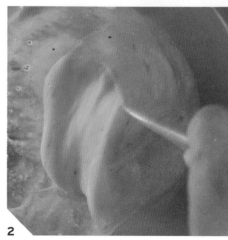

2

Omelette with potato crisps
Speedy tortilla

1. Peel the onion, halve it, cut it into strips and fry gently in a non-stick frying pan until translucent.

2. Break the eggs into a bowl, sprinkle with black pepper and beat with a fork.

3. Add the crisps and mix carefully.

4. Add the egg and crisp mixture to the onions.

5. Carefully crush the crisps with a fork so that the egg covers them and no spaces are left in the omelette when it's cooked. Turn the tortilla after 5 minutes and gently fry it for another 5 minutes.

Cut the finished tortilla into small pieces and serve on a plate with aioli (garlic mayonnaise) and a few green olives.

Favourite foods with a difference

 20

■ The tortilla will be easier to turn if you place a plate over the frying pan and tip the tortilla onto the plate. Then allow the tortilla to slide back into the pan.

2 large eggs

 50 g (1³/₄ oz) cornflakes

1 pinch of cinnamon

1

2

Sweet scrambled egg with cornflakes
Cornflakes in a frying pan

1. Beat the eggs with a fork and add 2 tablespoons of sugar.

2. Mix in the cornflakes briskly, so that they do not soften too much.

3. Melt 1 tablespoon of butter in a frying pan until it foams and then pour in the cornflake and egg mixture.

4. Leave to thicken into scrambled egg, stirring occasionally.

   Serve on plates and sprinkle with a little extra sugar and a pinch of cinnamon.

Favourite foods with a difference

 10

■ **Also tastes good without cornflakes or with other cereal flakes.**

3 small potatoes

 3 small sweet potatoes

 1/2 tsp ground cumin

1

2

Sweet potato pancake

African potato pancake

1. Peel the potatoes and sweet potatoes and grate coarsely with a kitchen grater.

2. In a bowl, season the grated potatoes with salt and ground cumin and mix well.

3. Heat 3 tablespoons of oil in a non-stick frying pan and add the grated potatoes.

4. Keep stirring the potato mass and pre-cook them slightly. As the potatoes will absorb a lot of oil,

add a little more oil to allow the pancake to become nice and crisp.

5. Shape the potatoes into a large, even pancake with a wooden spoon and fry for 5 minutes. Then turn and continue to fry for another 5 minutes.

Take out the pancake and cut it into pieces. This goes well with vegetables in a creamy sauce. It will serve 4 as an accompaniment.

Favourite foods with a difference

25

- It's easier to turn such a large pancake if you first place a plate over the frying pan and tip the whole thing upside down, and then slide the pancake back into the frying pan.

3

4

5

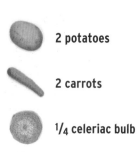 2 potatoes

 2 carrots

¼ celeriac bulb

1 sprig of rosemary

1 egg

1

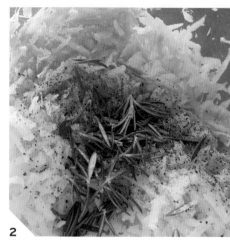
2

Potato and vegetable pancakes
Grate 'em small

1. Peel the potatoes, carrots and celeriac and grate coarsely into a bowl.

2. Strip off and add the rosemary leaves. Season with salt and black pepper.

3. Break the egg over the seasoned vegetables and mix together with a fork.

4. Heat 2 tablespoons of oil in a non-stick frying pan and make small round pancakes with a spoon.

5. Fry over a medium heat and turn after 5 minutes. The pancakes should be golden and crisp.

Now serve them on plates, with quick-fried meat or simple marinated salmon.

Favourite foods with a difference

■ **You can grate almost any firm vegetables, such as parsnips, fennel bulb, courgettes and many others, to make vegetable pancakes.**

3

4

5

300 g (10½ oz) skinless salmon fillet

 2 sesame seed buns

 2 tbsp rémoulade sauce

 1 tomato

 1 small onion

 8 slices of cucumber

1

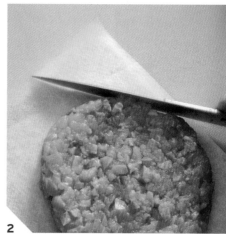

2

Salmon burger in a sesame bun with rémoulade sauce

Salmon burgers

1. Dice the salmon fillet into small cubes, then chop the cubes with a knife a few more times to dice the salmon more finely.

2. Put the chopped salmon onto waxed paper and shape two even, round burgers about 1 cm (½ inch) thick.

3. Place the burgers in a non-stick frying pan with 1 tablespoon of oil, pull out the waxed paper and fry the burgers on both sides for a total of 2–3 minutes.

4. Halve the sesame seed buns, toast them briefly and spread the bottom half of each with a little rémoulade sauce. Cover with slices of tomato and place the fried salmon burger on top.

5. Spread a little more rémoulade sauce on the salmon burgers. Cut the onion into rings. Put the onion rings and the slices of cucumber on top of the salmon burgers and crown with the tops of the sesame seed buns.

Lettuce leaves, red onions, cherry tomatoes and rocket also make good burger trimmings.

Favourite foods with a difference

* ** 15

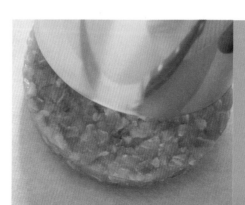

■ **Use a round mould to make beautiful, even burgers – that's what the professionals do!**

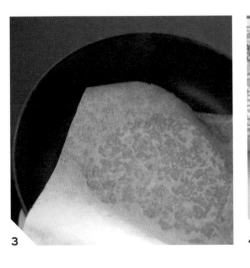

3

4

5

2 skinless chicken breasts

 2 eggs

 4 tbsp grated Parmesan cheese

 2 tbsp plain flour

Chicken breasts in a cheese and egg coating
Chicken in a Parmesan coat

1. Cut the chicken breasts diagonally into two halves, so that each makes two chicken steaks. Season with salt and pepper.

2. Beat the eggs with the Parmesan and spread the flour on a flat plate.

3. First, roll the chicken pieces in flour and then dip both sides in the egg and cheese mixture.

4. Heat 2 tablespoons of butter and 3 tablespoons of oil in a frying pan until foamy. Put the chicken pieces into the pan. After 2 minutes turn them carefully.

5. Make sure that the chicken pieces do not stick to the bottom of the pan and burn. After frying, taken them out and leave them to drain briefly on a paper towel.

Spread tomato sauce onto plates and place the pieces of chicken in their coating on top. Decorate with grated cheese. Serve with spaghetti, and make any child happy!

Favourite foods with a difference

25

■ For a very quick tomato sauce, bring some tomato juice to the boil and season with salt, black pepper and a pinch of sugar.

2 eggs

 1/2 tsp sweet paprika

 200 g (7 oz) potato crisps

 2 skinless chicken breasts

 2 tbsp plain flour

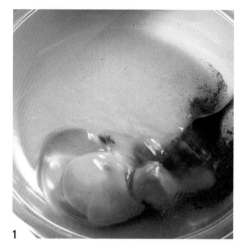

1

2

Chicken breasts coated with potato crisps
Crispy-crumbed chicken breast

1. Beat the eggs in a bowl with the paprika.

2. Put the potato crisps in a baking dish and crush finely (best done with a potato masher).

3. Cut the chicken breasts diagonally into two halves, season with salt and pepper and roll them in the plain flour. Then dip them in the beaten egg and finally roll them in the crushed crisps.

4. Heat 3 tablespoons of oil and 2 tablespoons of butter in a frying pan. Adding the oil means that the butter will not burn so quickly.

5. Now fry the chicken on both sides in the pan, 2-3 minutes a side, until golden.

Arrange on plates and serve with cucumber salad, parsley potatoes or simply with a spicy tomato sauce.

Favourite foods with a difference

■ **You can of course use flavoured crisps, but in that case leave out the paprika.**

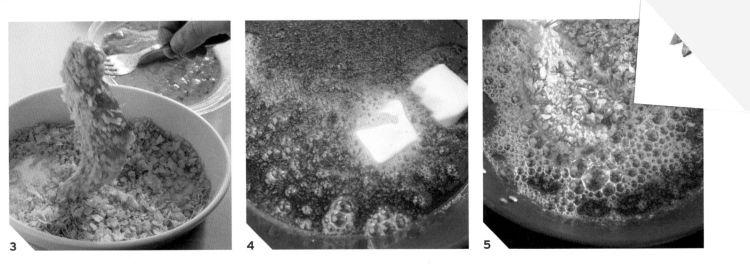

3

4

5

2 skinless chicken breasts

 2 tbsp plain flour

 1 egg

 150 g (5¹/₄ oz) crushed cornflakes

1

2

Chicken breasts in cornflake coating
Cornflakes well done

1. Halve the chicken breasts lengthways and season with salt and pepper.

2. Roll them in flour and dip them in the beaten egg with a fork.

3. Roll them in the crushed cornflakes and gently press on the cornflake crumbs to make them stick.

4. In a frying pan, heat 3 tablespoons of vegetable oil and 2 tablespoons of butter until foamy and then fry the chicken pieces on both sides.

5. Leave to drain briefly on a paper towel.

Serve with buttered peas or carrots as an accompaniment.

Favourite foods with a difference

 ✳
✳ 25
✳

■ **To crush the cornflakes in a bowl, use the underside of a pepper mill. Cornflakes make the chicken coating super-crispy – a guaranteed hit for children's birthdays.**

3

4

5

 3 potatoes

 2 tbsp plain flour

2 eggs

 1 tbsp soured cream

1/2 apple

1

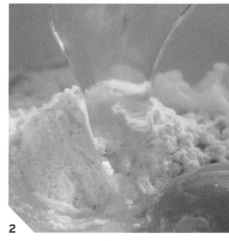

2

Potato pancake with apple

Skinny potato strudel

1. Peel the potatoes and use a fine grater to grate them into a bowl.

2. Add the flour and the eggs.

3. Add the soured cream and stir to make a smooth batter.

4. Remove the core of the apple and slice it. In a frying pan, heat 2 tablespoons of oil and 1 tablespoon of butter and add

half the potato batter. Distribute the apple slices on top of the potato pancake and cover with the rest of the potato batter.

5. After 4 minutes turn the pancake and fry gently for another 3 minutes.

Take out the pancake and serve. Sprinkle with sugar if desired.

Favourite foods with a difference

✳
✳ **25**
✳

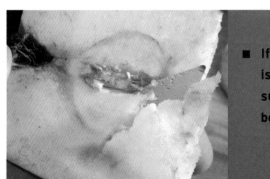

■ If you have half an apple that is turning brown on the cut surface, cut the brown part off before using it.

3

4

5

8 marshmallows

2 bread rolls

2 large tbsp chocolate-hazelnut spread

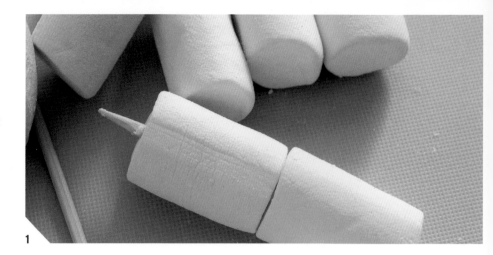
1

Marshmallow rolls with chocolate-hazelnut spread
For a sweet tooth

1. Thread the marshmallows onto cocktail sticks, 2 to each cocktail stick.

2. Halve the rolls and spread one half of each roll with a thick blob of the chocolate-hazelnut spread.

3. Carefully toast the marshmallow sticks over a gas flame and then immediately place them on the lower halves of the bread rolls. Cover with the other halves of the rolls and remove the sticks. Eat while still warm.

A very tasty snack.

Favourite foods with a difference

2

3

2 ripe apples

 60 g (2¹/₄ oz) shelled walnuts

 4 tbsp brown sugar

 1 ready-made shortcrust pastry

 150 g (5¹/₄ oz) soured cream

1

2

Apple tart with walnuts and soured cream
Fallen fruits

1. Peel the apples, quarter them and cut out the cores with a knife. Roughly chop the shelled walnuts.

2. Put apples and walnuts into a bowl and sprinkle with the brown sugar. Mix and leave to draw for 5 minutes.

3. Put the shortcrust pastry onto a baking tray covered with baking paper. Arrange the apples on the base, leaving an uncovered border of about 3 cm (1¹/₄ inch) all around. Stir the soured cream and pour it over the apples.

4. Now press the tart base's edge in towards the centre and once more sprinkle the apples with brown sugar.

Put in the oven, preheated to 220°C (425°F/Gas Mark 7), and bake for 25-30 minutes. Leave to cool a little.

Best served warm.

Favourite foods with a difference

✳
✳
✳ 45

■ Sprinkle the pastry edge with a little brown sugar as well to make sure it turns golden brown.

3

4

150 g (5½ oz) muesli

 60 g (2¼ oz) plain flour

 1 egg

 400 g (14 oz) drained canned fruit salad

1

2

Muesli cake
My first cake

1. Put the muesli into a bowl with the flour, 3 tablespoons of sugar and 2 tablespoons of butter.

2. Use your hands to mix all the ingredients. Add the egg and quickly work it in.

3. Spread a portion of the fruit salad over the bottom of a baking dish. Spread some of the muesli crumble over the top. Continue in layers until the dish is full.

4. Finally, place a few more pieces of fruit on top of the muesli crumble. Preheat the oven to 210°C (410°F/ Gas Mark 6) and bake for about 20 minutes.

   Take out the cake, sprinkle with caster sugar and serve.

Favourite foods with a difference

25

3

4

What can I cook?

Index of basic ingredients

How much time do I have? Recipes in order of preparation and cooking times